POEMS OF FAITH
& INSPIRATION

JOYCE FOLSOM JOHNSON

To God be the glory.

from

Joyce Folsom Johnson

authorHOUSE®

AuthorHouse™
1663 Liberty Drive
Bloomington, IN 47403
www.authorhouse.com
Phone: 1 (800) 839-8640

Published by AuthorHouse 05/18/2017

ISBN: 978-1-5246-9254-4 (sc)
ISBN: 978-1-5246-9253-7 (e)

Library of Congress Control Number: 2017907790

Scripture quotations marked KJV are from the Holy Bible, King James Version (Authorized Version). First published in 1611. Quoted from the KJV Classic Reference Bible, Copyright © 1983 by The Zondervan Corporation.

Scripture quotations marked NIV are taken from the Holy Bible, New International Version®. NIV®. Copyright © 1973, 1978, 1984 by International Bible Society. Used by permission of Zondervan. All rights reserved. [Biblica]

About the Author

By Marcia Lee Johnson Newell

In Shapleigh, Maine, during the Autumn of 1939, Joyce Elizabeth Folsom Johnson was born in the same farmhouse her mother had been born in, as had generations before them. Her family had a strong literary heritage with Donald Parker Folsom as her father and her mother, Beulah Olive Pillsbury Folsom. She was a treasured child amongst an extended family of adults.

Joyce grew up, married her husband, Ernest, and together they raised a family in Massachusetts. Many of her poems are drawn from that family life.

She started writing later in life after the hubbub of raising children had subsided some. Joyce describes her first poem, "Sidewalk Smile," below.

"This was the first poem that ever came to me when I was sleeping soundly. I awoke and the poem was still whirling around in my mind. I was exhausted, but intrigued and amused, so I dragged myself out of bed, went downstairs still half asleep and bleary-eyed, fumbled around for a paper and pencil, and wrote it down because I knew I would never remember it in the morning.. .. I had no way of knowing that this was the beginning of many more such instances when my sleep would be interrupted by this "nudging" from the Lord to get up and write."

Joyce later adds, "If your life has been blessed by only one of these poems, then my work and the help of my family, shall not have been in vain."

"Joyce Folsom Johnson, daughter of Donald and Beulah Pillsbury Folsom, is a graduate of Sanford High School and Nasson College in Springvale, Maine. She served as private Medical Secretary for Dr. Ralph Belmont, Sanford, ME., and Dr. Graves at the University of Maine, Orono, Maine. She is the mother of three, Marcia, Dean, and Christine, and the grandmother of nine. "Joyce experienced enough of practical life, along with its "ups and downs", to become well-qualified to impart her faith and wisdom through speech, prose, and poetry. For over half a century, she has inspired others, as much through her daily lifestyle, as by her poems."

Ernest M, Johnson, Engineering Physicist-Retired

Table of Contents

AGING

This poem came to me at 11:00 at night in October of 1993, which is well past my usual bedtime. I had said my evening prayer but couldn't get to sleep because of what had happened earlier that day. The "urging" to write became so strong that I once again had to leave a warm comfortable bed when I felt too tired to do so. As usual, when the Holy Spirit "nudges" me, the poem flowed onto the paper as fast as I could write it down.

The incident that had bothered me earlier in the day and inspired this poem, happened while Ernie and I were visiting at a nursing home. A gentleman visitor came along and was talking very politely to us. We were having a nice conversation. Suddenly, one of the Alzheimer patients, who could be quite annoying by asking the same question over and over, came up to us with her usual question, asking where her husband was. The man interrupted his polite conversation with us and shouted at her, "Get out of here!" This just kept bothering me until I got out of bed to write the poem entitled, "Please Be Patient."

Please Be Patient

Please be patient with me today.
I haven't always been this way.
I once was a child, so small and sweet,
With happy hands and dancing feet.

Then I grew up, still having fun,
And fell in love with a special one.
I raised my children so happily
And loved to bounce them on my knee.

As they grew up, the time flew by.
I hardly even blinked an eye,
When suddenly I saw myself
With faltering steps and failing health.

My eyes, once bright, are not too clear;
My ears, once sharp, can hardly hear;
My hands, once busy, are mostly bored;
My dancing feet will dance no more.

My mind, once keen, is now confused.
It hurts when people seem amused.
The person that you're seeing now,
I have become, I know not how.

Please be patient with me today.
I haven't always been this way.
It's not the way I hoped I'd be.

What you're seeing is not the real me.

This body I live in is wearing out,
But that's no reason for you to shout.
The person I am, is my soul within.
For you to mistreat me would be a sin.

Our Lord taught us all the Golden Rule.
Treat me right; please don't be cruel.
Be kind in what you say and do.
Before you know it, this could be you.

This poem was written in ten minutes on May 19, 1995, after visiting our good friend. He has multiple sclerosis and is confined to a wheelchair. He is hardly able to move and is unable to speak.

Trapped Inside My Body

Trapped in my body,
I just want to shout,
"My mind is still active.
Please let me out!"

Trapped in my body,
I just want to scream,
"Please let me out
To follow my dream."

Trapped in my body,
I don't want to stay
Sitting here quietly
Day after day.

Trapped in my body,
I remember my past,
When healthy and active
And moving so fast.

Trapped in my body,
This thought's in my mind:
"Where is the peace that
I'm longing to find?"

Trapped in my body,
I'm asking, "Why me?"
Then I think about Jesus
Who died on that tree.

For my forgiveness,
He went to the cross.
His undeserved suffering
Was so I won't be lost.

Trapped in my body,
I need not be alone.
I need not fear or worry.
I need not fret or moan.

For if I simply ask Him,
He'll live within my heart
And bear my burden with me.
My fears will then depart.

He said, "My yoke is easy
And My burden is light."
He'll be in that yoke with me
Helping carry it day and night.

And, if I just believe,
Eternal Life He'll give.
With a brand new body,
In Heaven I'll live.

Trapped in my body,
What can I do each day?
The greatest work of all
For others I can pray!

The Nursing Home

I now reside in a nursing home,
Sitting here silently, feeling alone.
The person who sleeps in the bed next to me--
I don't even know him. He doesn't know me.

Most of my possessions were given away.
I don't even have them to brighten my day.
I'm now crowded into this small little room.
My heart is so heavy with sadness and gloom.

I'm missing my loved ones so much every day.
They come by quite often, but can't always stay.
They really are busy with their own young lives,
Caring for their children, these husbands and wives.

My body grew old and would not allow me
To stay in my home where I wanted to be.
I'm much too disabled for my loved ones to give
The care that is needed, so it's here I must live.

My life was so happy when I was young and gay,
And now it is slipping so quickly away.
The days just drag on filled with sadness and pain,
And each new tomorrow brings more of the same.

From this phase of life there is no escaping.
I cannot go back. My heart's nearly breaking.
I know that from here, the next phase is dying.
Sometimes, when I think of it, I feel like crying.

But my faith is strong. I'll cling to Jesus' hand.
I know He'll escort me to His promised land.
I'll live there forever, never again to be alone.
When gently, He takes me from this nursing home.

"Why Didn't I Listen?"

"Why didn't I listen?"
I've heard people say.
Now that I'm older,
I think it every day.

When I was a child,
I'd listen to my dad
Who'd tell me the stories
Of when he was a lad.

Then I would also
Listen to my mom
Telling the tales
Of the things she had done.

Many times they told me
Of their genealogies.
They were very proud
Of their family trees.

I thought I had listened,
But in time, I forgot--
I hadn't paid full attention
To these things they had taught.

Now that they are gone,
Every day I yearn
To ask them my questions--
Their history to learn.

I'm now one of those seniors
Who are wanting to share
All that we have learned.
We want our loved ones to care.

But we see that glazed look
When we try to explain
Their history to them.
We know we're talking in vain.

They just don't understand
That someday they'll long
To ask us their questions,
But we will be gone.

God, too, must be frustrated
When He sees our eyes grow dim.
That's when it becomes obvious
We're not listening to Him.

But there is one great difference,
As our lives go on:
When we look to God for answers,
He will never be gone!

CLASS REUNIONS

This poem was written in June of 1992, as our Sanford, Maine, high school Class of 1957 reunion was approaching. When I was sending in our reservations, I was inspired to write this poem and include it, not knowing what, if anything, would be done with it. When I got to the reunion, my poem was framed and displayed on the front table.

<u>SHS Class of 1957 35th Reunion</u>

Here it is, that time again.
For this Reunion number ten,
Fifteen, twenty, or twenty-five?
No! Good grief! It's thirty-five!

I pause to think and want to know:
Where indeed did that time go?
When time flies by, so I've been told,
It's a sign that we are growing old!

Growing old? But can that be
What's happening to you and me?
Is that why we're getting fat,
Gray, wrinkled, bald, and all of that?

Our bodies will not always do
All that we expect them to.
And there are things that we forget.
But, luckily, it's not bad yet.

There are many reasons I like this age,
And they could fill another page.
There's life and joy with those we love,
And blessings from our God above.

And one of the very nicest parts
Is grandchildren born to fill our hearts
With love overflowing, pure and sweet.
Yes, growing old can be really neat!

So here's to Reunion thirty-five.
We're grateful and happy to be alive.
Let's all relax and enjoy the party,
And God willing, return for number forty!

SHS Class of 1957 50th Reunion

Our class reunion is coming.
It's reunion number fifty!
Seeing all of our classmates
Will really be quite nifty!

Oh, no! The old insecurities
Start to creep in from everywhere,
The ones left over from high school,
Which we thought were no longer there:

"We're overweight. We're looking old.
What about our hair?
What will all of our classmates think?
What are we going to wear?

"What have we accomplished
Since we left Sanford High?
Have we fulfilled our dreams?
What else should we have tried?"

So, now I'd like to share with you
What I've learned along the way:
None of these things really matter.
God loves us anyway!

Because He loves each one of us,
We've no need to feel inferior;
And since He loves us equally,
We must never feel superior.

Knowing this, why should we fret
About what others think or say?
This knowledge is one of His special gifts
Bringing comfort every day.

So, as we count our blessings,
We can relax and realize
It will be fun to attend our reunion and
Share the blessings in each other's lives.

SHS Class of 1957 55th Reunion

It's the third reunion poem
I've written through the years.
Each reunion has brought us
Some laughter, some tears.

This year our reunion
Is number fifty-five.
We're grateful to God
That we're still alive.

We've become grandparents.
We're old, and we're gray,
Fat, wrinkled, and sagging
More every day!

Our bodies are older.
They ache, and they creak.
Our strength is waning.
We get tired and weak.

Our memories draw blanks
And are getting short.
Some hairlines recede.
Most bellies are "pot".

Our vision's diminished.
Our hearing is going.
Our list of complaints
Just keeps on growing.

But we're grateful to God
Just to be here
To share our laughter,
To share our tears,

To share our memories
(If we can remember!)
Of the fun we had when
School began each September.

We'll enjoy time together
Till this reunion ends
And be grateful to God
For our old high school friends!

FAITH

This poem came to me while I was at our camp looking out over the beauty of the morning mist lifting off Square Pond, surrounded by fall foliage and listening to a praise song on WSEW 88.5 FM on the radio. I was moved to tears, asking myself, "How can anyone not believe?" Also, I had been praying for inspiration for a Christmas poem and asking people for some ideas. When I got to the sixth verse, I realized that I had just been given my Christmas poem!

How Can Anyone Not Believe?

How can anyone not believe
When this wondrous world we see?
Its seasons, its colors, its lakes and seas
Just open our eyes and see.

How can anyone not believe
With order all around?
The heavens at night for all to see
Yes, order does abound.

How can anyone not believe
As we think of the universe?
No "accident" could this possibly be
That assumption couldn't be worse!

How can anyone not believe
When we think about our life?
The awe when a newborn starts to breathe,
To explain it, we can't even try.

How can anyone not believe
With all the care we are given?
Yes, God is guiding you and me
As well as all the heavens.

How can anyone not believe
That our Lord came down to earth?
In the form of Jesus, He came that we
Could have life and hope in His birth.

How can anyone not believe
That He died for our sins in our place?
Accepting His forgiveness will give us peace.
Believe and live in His grace!

The inspiration for this poem, which was written on November 13, 1993, came while watching television. As usual, the people on television were making a big deal out of Friday, the 13th. On this particular day, they were especially worried because Friday, the 13th was happening on the same day as a full moon. I was disgusted by all of the fuss they were making and was inspired to write the following poem.

Superstitions

As Christians, we have often heard:
We must not be superstitious.
Our lives are governed by God's Word
And He is never vicious.

He doesn't sit upon His throne
In Heaven way up high
And send bad luck down on His own
Because black cats walk by!

He doesn't give to any of us
(I cannot make it clearer)
Seven years of terrible luck
Because we break a mirror!

He doesn't strike our loved ones dead
(He's not a mean old fella)
When inside a building, we feel led
To put up our umbrella!

Is walking under ladders such
A dangerous condition?
Yes, some tools might fall on us;
Not because of superstition.

When we're walking down the street
And step upon a crack,
Our heart must not miss a single beat,
We won't "break our mother's back"!

Friday the 13th is the day
That people always fear,
But it's not different in any way
From other days of the year.

The 13th, like all the 365,
Belongs to God above.
That day He doesn't threaten the lives
Of us or those we love.

We must not read our horoscope
Our fate's not in the stars.
In Jesus only is our hope
Not in Jupiter or Mars!

Our Lord has given us His guide
And that's our Bible dear.
We only have to look inside
For what we need to hear.

Nowhere in His precious Word,
As you have, no doubt, guessed,
Have any of these things occurred.
Lay superstitions to rest!

My Road Maps

When those I love have traveled,
As they've done on many a day,
I've drawn them countless road maps
To help them find their way.

It seems that I'm the person
Who makes maps for all occasions,
Guiding people on their way
To get to their destinations.

For two weddings, I drew the maps,
Complete with full directions,
Which guided the many guests
From the weddings to the receptions.

When our church held its baptism
At our cottage at the lake,
My maps were used to guide folks
Showing them the roads to take.

After giving people my maps,
I always wait and pray
That my maps had no mistakes
Causing people to lose their way.

The longer until their arrival,
The more concerned I get
If I have arrived where we're going
And they are not there yet.

This causes me to pause
And think about my life:
The way I'm living as daughter,
Mother, grandmother and wife.

My life must be a road map
For all who look to me
To set for them an example
Of how their lives should be.

With my maps I guide them
As they travel on their way.
With my life I pray I'll guide
So they won't go astray.

I pray that I will never
Take a step, no, none at all,
That my loved ones should not follow
Or would cause them to stumble and fall.

I must tell them about Jesus.
His life for us He gave.
His blood was shed to forgive our sins
Our eternal lives to save.

They must know that when we sin,
It's as though we hold the nail
And once more drive it through His flesh...
But He forgives us when we fail.

And when we have been forgiven,
We experience such release
From the bondage of guilt we've been
        carrying.
Our lives are filled with peace.

They must know God gives equal love
To all His children each one.
We must not feel superior to others
And should feel inferior to none.

Then 'till we're all in Heaven,
Until we are safely Home,
I'll pray that all will arrive there,
Nevermore to roam.

The map that I will give them
Is Jesus, the Life, Truth and Way.
For eternal life in Heaven,
Believe and receive Him today.

His Healing Touch

Kneeling as I always do
Before I go to bed,
I said my nightly prayers and faced
Another night of dread.

My shoulder had been filled with pain
That night and many before.
How I wished the pain would stop
And bother me no more.

The doctor's shot had worked last week
For just a day or two,
And then the pain came back again.
I didn't know what to do.

I decided that I'd ask the Lord
To take away the pain.
He answered and I felt it leave.
It has not come back again!

I now know the meaning of Gaither's song
That I have loved so much.
He Touched Me means much more because
I've felt God's healing touch.

On June 16, 1996, I was awakened at daybreak at our camp on Square Pond in Shapleigh, Maine, by the many birds singing outside our open windows. I wrote this poem in fifteen minutes.

God's Alarm Clocks

At the dawning of every new day
We don't really need a clock.
An alarm is sounded right away
By the "cockadoodledo" of the cock.

Many other birds join the chorus
And cheerfully sing along.
They say to each other, "Please join us
As we happily sing our song."

Some of their songs are perky.
Some of them mourn and coo.
Even the "gobbling" turkey
Is saying, "Good morning to you."

The baby birds are all squawking
For their very first meal of the day.
To their parents they are talking
Saying, "Get up and get on your way!"

The chipmunks' voices are "chipping,"
Adding their sounds to the morn.
While back and forth they go zipping,
They seem happy that they were born.

Most of the birds' songs are pleasing;
Some more than others, I'd say.
But surely our Lord is teasing
When He sends the loud crows our way!

We hear the gray squirrels go running
On the roof above our room;
And, as we approach the dawning,
We hear the loud cry of the loon.

What a special way to wake us,
Our Lord has carefully planned.
All is designed to make us
A contented woman or man.

I just experienced another one of God's "non-coincidences"!

Last year, I was inspired to write a poem entitled, THE SUN CAME SHINING THROUGH, about some beautiful forsythia shrubs which I had driven by on my way to my daughter, Marcia Newell's, house in Litchfield, NH. I didn't know the people's names who lived in the house where the forsythia shrubs were located, but I wanted them to have a copy of the poem because it was written about their shrubs. I was, however, a bit apprehensive because I didn't know them or how they would accept the poem.

During the following year, I had planned to take the poem to their house and leave it in the newspaper box beside their mailbox. I kept forgetting to do it; and everytime I drove by their house, I was reminded of it and was determined to do it the next time I went to visit Marcia. One time I went to Marcia's with a piece of paper on which to write them a note explaining how the poem came about and who I was visiting in Litchfield, and an envelope in which to put the poem and note; but I then found that I had forgotten to bring the poem! Another time I went there with everything; but when I looked at the poem, there was a grease spot on it which I hadn't noticed before.

Last week, I was determined that I would definitely have the poem and letter with me to leave at their house the following Friday when we would be going to Marcia's to babysit our granddaughter, Bethany. I went over the poem once more, changed words, phrases, added words and thought I finally had it ready. Yesterday was Friday, and we were in a rush to get out of our house at 7:30 a.m. to get to Marcia's in time for her to go to work. I looked at the poem and couldn't believe that there was another tiny spot on this one after it had been on the kitchen counter overnight. Ernie said it hardly showed; but, to me, it looked less than perfect, so I rushed to our computer and made a fresh copy.

When we were driving past the home where the forsythia shrubs are located, we saw a gentleman preparing to get into his car. Ernie said, "Do you want to stop and give the poem to him?" I was too nervous and said, "No." Then I changed my mind; but we had already gone past their house and were running late, so we didn't go back.

On our way home yesterday afternoon, we stopped and left the poem and the note in their newspaper box. I kept wondering about it after that. "Would they notice it in there?" "Would they not see it, and would it get wet being out all night in the rain that was forecast?" "How would they react?" Last night, when it was raining, I thought about the poem again and wondered if they had found it. Today I thought about it only a couple of times. "Would I ever know whether or not they had found it?" I didn't think about it anymore, because it was in God's hands anyway. He had given it to me, and He wanted me to give it to them.

This afternoon, Marcia called with the following story to tell me: This morning they had taken their dog to a rabies clinic in their town. The lady who was taking the information noticed that Marcia's last name was Newell. She said, "Newell? Do you live on Wren Street.?" Marcia said she did. The lady said, "I had a lovely poem in my box from your mother!" She said that she really liked it and would like to share it with others. Marcia told her that she felt sure it would be fine with me. It turns out that she is a teacher at Griffin Memorial School where Marcia's oldest daughter, Bonnie, attended for one and one half years after they moved to Litchfield in 1996. Bonnie is now in Litchfield Middle School.

God is so good!!! He knew I had been wondering about the poem. He put this lady and Marcia together for the first time ever in order that Marcia could call and tell me that the poem had been received and appreciated. This reinforces once more the definition of a coincidence that I heard on Dr. D. James Kennedy's Coral Ridge Ministries television program: "Coincidence: A miracle in which God chooses to be anonymous!"

The Sun Came Shining Through

This morning, while driving north on a road,
I was really enjoying the ride.
Springtime was bursting forth everywhere.
The weather was warm outside.

The grayness of winter was being replaced
With spring colors on bushes and trees;
But, in spite of the colors, they looked a bit dull
As they swayed back and forth in the breeze.

I then made a right turn and headed east.
What I saw took my breath away!
A row of forsythia shrubs standing there
Were illuminated by the sun's rays.

The sun was beyond them, away in the east;
But its light was shining through.
It looked just as if they were all ablaze
With the brightest yellow hue!

The other bushes and trees came to life--
Bright red buds and new leaves of green.
The sun shining through these bushes and trees
Was the prettiest I'd ever seen

I couldn't stop thinking of the difference it made
When the sun came shining through.
The beauty and new life it gave to this scene
Changed it all to a bright shining hue.

The same thing is true of what happens to folks
When, by the Spirit, they're born anew.
When they ask God's Son, Jesus, into their lives,
He changes them and makes them new.

Their lives are changed in such beautiful ways.
They're made fresh as the morning dew.
Their sins are forgiven. They "radiate" with peace
When the Son is shining through!

This was written on September 3, 1996, after visiting Evelyn Waterhouse and her son, Wayne, who was visiting at her home on Square Pond in Shapleigh, Maine. While Wayne was outdoors, his dog, Scamper, was frantically jumping back and forth from each piece of furniture in front of the windows, searching for a sight of Wayne.

Scamper Found Her Master

Today, a little dog named Scamper
Was frantically searching around.
Back and forth she kept pacing--
Up onto the couch and down.

Behind the couch was a window
That the little dog could look out;
But each time she left the window,
All she could do was pout.

Her master had gone outside.
Scamper felt she was all alone.
Three other dogs didn't matter--
Neither did a bone!

She kept roaming here and there,
Searching at every turn.
She needed to find her master.
Oh, how her heart did yearn.

She jumped on the couch one more time--
Again looked out the window.
This time her tail started wagging!
Her face was all aglow!

She'd finally found her master,
The one she'd been searching for.
Now she could be at peace.
Her heart would yearn no more.

That's how it is with people.
We roam and search everywhere,
Trying to fill a void,
Looking for someone to care.

We need to find our Master,
The One Who loves us so.
No one could love us more--
He died for us, you know.

He went to the cross in our place,
For the forgiveness of our sins.
He'll come into our hearts
If we'll just ask Him in.

Once we have found our Master,
We no longer suffer defeat.
We no longer have a void.
Like Scamper, our lives are complete.

The Two of You in "Counted Cross Stitch"

I've lovingly stitched the names
Of you and the one you love--
Each of you sent to the other
By our dear Lord above.

I've also stitched the cross
To remind everyone who comes near
That our dear Savior died
For each person listed here.

None other could love us more
Than to die on the cross in our place
To forgive us of our sins
So we can live in His grace.

All you have to do is believe
And invite Christ into your heart.
Eternal Life will be yours.
Believing loved ones will never part.

This poem was written early in the morning of August 5, 1996, after I rescued a spider from the sink at our camp on Square Pond in Shapleigh, Maine. I think of the same thing I wrote about in the poem each time I rescue an insect and set it free.

The Spider in Our Sink

This morning I rescued a spider
Which was stranded in our sink.
It looked as though it had been there
The whole night long, I think.

The spider seemed exhausted
From trying not to drown,
Climbing the sides of the sink,
Repeatedly falling back down.

I extended to him a napkin
For him to climb upon,
But he kept running away.
The conflict went on and on.

Into the napkin, I trapped him
And took him safely outside.
He didn't know had I left him
In the sink, he'd have surely died.

This scene brought to mind a person
Striving to save himself,
Climbing and repeatedly falling,
Continually refusing help.

Our Lord must feel like I did
When the spider kept running from me.
He's longing for us to reach out
So He can set us free.

Free from the sins that bind us,
From our shame that weighs heavily,
Free to become a Christian
And to live on eternally.

All we must do is trust
And, with faith, believe in Him.
He's waiting for us to reach out--
He'll rescue and save us from sin.

This poem came to me on October 14, 1994, while sitting alone in the dark on the porch of our camp at Square Pond in Shapleigh, ME, looking at the lights reflecting on the lake from various distances.

Lights Reflecting on the Lake

As I sit here on our porch at night
On the shore of this lovely lake,
I'm in awe as I look at a single light
And the reflection it can make.

A light across the cove sends a ray
Upon the water I see.
Its reflection reaches all the way
To the shore in front of me.

Farther away is an island where
There is still another light.
Its rays also reach this shore from there
To brighten up the night.

Across the lake, which amazes me more,
'Cause it's over a mile away,
A single light can be seen from this shore
Along with its tiny ray.

This holds a lesson for us to find
As along life's way we go:
We don't know how far our light will shine
To people we don't even know.

Little things that we do or say,
Whether they're good or bad,
Can reach those both near and far away
And make them happy or sad.

Our Lord, Who is the Source of all light,
Sent us His Light through His Son
To brighten up the day and the night
Of all whom we meet--every one.

The Missing Piece of the Puzzle

Our bodies are like a puzzle
With thousands and thousands of parts.
God knits them all together when
He forms us 'neath our mother's heart.

He unites the cells from our parents
In a tiny little space
And knits our bodies together
With each part in its place.

How this process happens,
Only our Savior knows
The way He creates our fingers
And all of our tiny toes.

Every single part of
Our bodies is formed so fine
In our mother's womb in secret
As it says in Psalm 139.

After the Lord forms our bodies,
And at the time of our birth,
He breathes life into us
As we're welcomed here on earth.

But one thing is always missing
In each puzzle that He creates:
He leaves a God-shaped void
In each person that He makes.

It is a special void
He waits for us to fill
Because He gives to us
Something He calls free will.

This is an empty void
That we can never fill
With any earthly thing.
Nothing ever will.

We search the wide world over
Trying everything,
But nothing satisfies
That longing deep within.

Only Jesus is the answer
That will fill that God-shaped part.
He'll satisfy that longing
When we ask Him into our heart.

After we have done this,
We have peace that is so sweet.
There'll be no more frantic searching.
At last we will be complete.

An Outcast

When I was born,
I was lovely to behold.
Created by God,
I was humble, not bold.

In my God-given beauty,
I stood straight and tall.
I was wonderfully made,
God's blessing for all.

All children loved me.
I was special to them.
To their mothers they'd take me
Time and again.

But, as the years passed,
People started to frown,
Look unkindly at me
And "put me down".

I was no longer loved
As a blessing from God.
They made me an outcast
Which saddened our Lord.

If they would take time
To really look at me,
They'd be surprised
At the beauty they'd see.

But that's how folks are--
They don't always see
The miracle God made.
A blessing I should be!

For I'm a dandelion
As pretty as can be,
But lots of folks hate me
And label me a weed.

I could make them smile
In their times of need,
And I could nourish them
If on my greens they'd feed.

But they want to kill me.
Thinking I'm a disgrace,
They make sure only grass
Can stand in my place.

That's how it is with people
They even hate their own,
Putting people down
Till they're left all alone.

But God created all.
He loves each one the same.
Society puts them down.
"Outcast" is their name.

We must love all flowers.
God created every one.
And we must love all people
As we are loved by God's Son.

His was the greatest love
That has ever been shown--
The death of our dear Savior
To save all His own.

He died for the sins of all
On a cross in our place.
If we'll believe in Him,
We'll live forever in His grace.

The Most Important Choice You'll Ever Make

Will you be in Heaven with those you've
loved,
Christian loved ones who've gone before?
Do you miss them sorely and want to be
With them forevermore?

This is the question to ask yourself
While you're still here on earth:
Do you want to be with your loved ones or
friends
Or a child to whom you gave birth?

Eternal Life will be given to you.
Where you'll spend it, you must choose.
It can be spent in Heaven so dear,
Or in Hell where everything you'll lose.

The Bible is very clear on this.
The fires of Hell are real.
You can spend eternity there,
And its torment you will feel.

But our Lord Jesus gave us the choice
If we will believe in Him.
Each of us must be born again
And He'll take away our sin.

Please don't be fooled into thinking you can
Get to Heaven by being good.
Believing in Jesus and receiving God's
grace
Is the only way anyone could.

"I am the way, the truth, and the life."
In John 14: 6, you see,
Jesus says, "No one comes to the Father
Except through me."

We must believe that He came to earth,
God in the form of a man,
To give us Eternal Life in Heaven
According to His plan.

He took our sins upon Himself
As He hung on that terrible cross.
For all of our sins he bled and died
So we would not be lost.

Because Jesus died and rose again,
The grave will not be our goal.
He doesn't promise to save our body,
But He promises to save our soul.

When we believe that He died for us
And ask Him our sins to forgive,
He'll give us such incredible peace
While here on earth we live.

Then, when it's time for us to die,
If we've asked Him into our heart,
Eternal Life in Heaven He'll give.
Believing loved ones will never part.

When We're Tempted to Sin

For those of us who love Jesus
And have Him in our hearts,
We must look to Him for guidance.
In sin we must take no part!

For our Savior died to save us,
To forgive us of our sin.
But Satan keeps on tempting us
And trying to lure us in.

Whenever we get tempted
As we travel along God's way,
We must quickly look to Jesus
Who will help us not to stray.

For Jesus took our beating
And died for us on the cross
For the forgiveness of our sins,
So we would not be lost.

He was wounded in His body
In very specific parts.
He saved us from those wounds
When we asked Him into our hearts.

On His head a crown of thorns
Was placed, and there He bled.
When we're tempted to sin in our thoughts,
We must think of His wounded head.

That very same crown of thorns
Caused His blood to flow down to His eyes.
When our eyes are tempted to sin,
We must think of His blood-filled eyes.

His hands were nailed to the cross
According to God's plan.
When our hands are tempted to sin,
We must think of His wounded hands.

His body was pierced with a spear
After He had died.
When our bodies are tempted to sin,
We must think of His wounded side.

On the cross, huge spikes were driven
Through the flesh of Jesus' feet.
When we're tempted to walk into sin,
We must think of His wounded feet.

Satan will always tempt us,
But Jesus will help us to win.
If we'll quickly look to Jesus,
He'll help us resist the sin.

Please Don't Cry

My body's so tired,
So racked with pain.
I'm longing to go back to
God from Whom I came.

For there, He will wipe
Every tear from my eye.
There'll be no more pain,
No more need to cry.

My Jesus will meet me
When this body I leave.
He'll carry me safely,
So please do not grieve.

If you were in Heaven
And we loved ones remained,
For us, you would surely
Ask the same.

A new body I'll have when
I leave my "earthly tent".
I'll live in it forever,
Pain free and content.

When a seed is planted,
It also has to die
Before its living plant
Can reach up to the sky.

Our bodies are like seeds;
And, like seeds, they, too, must die
To be raised a spiritual body
And live forever on high.

I'll be there happily waiting
In Heaven up above
Until I'm reunited
With those on earth I love.

So please believe in Jesus,
And ask Him into your heart.
That's what you all must do
So we will never part.

The Peepers' Chorus

The way that we know
It is finally spring
Is when the "peepers"
Begin to sing.

As nighttime falls,
They start their song
And happily sing it
All night long.

One starts to peep,
Then two, three, and four.
Before we know it,
There are hundreds more.

Their song is loud.
It keeps on growing.
It seems like their hearts
Are overflowing.

Then all of a sudden,
The music stops
As though the conductor's
Baton has dropped!

In unison they all
Have stopped their peeping.
We start to wonder
If perhaps they're sleeping.

Then suddenly we hear
One tiny peep--
Shyly and quietly,
So soft and sweet.

Then one joins in,
Then two, three, and four;
And once again,
There are hundreds more!

This pattern's repeated
All through the night
Till morning comes
With the sun so bright.

God's rhythms and patterns
Become very clear
As we welcome the
"Peepers' Chorus" each year.

God's Instructions to Noah

God said to Noah,
"Go build an ark."
Noah obeyed and
Worked dawn till dark.

He worked many days.
He worked many nights.
God gave him instructions
So he'd do it right.

The people all laughed
While Noah built the ark
From resinous wood
Which he sealed with tar.

While building, Noah noticed
That there would be no sail
To blow the ark along
When the winds prevailed.

He also may have wondered
Why there'd be no steering wheel
With which to steer the ark
When it began to keel.

Noah surely noticed
That the ark would have no rudder
To guide it on its course
Going one way and the other.

There would be no motor
To move the ark along.
(What could God be thinking?
Wasn't this all wrong?)

But Noah never questioned.
He was a man of faith.
He knew that God would guide him
For he lived in His grace.

It was as if the Lord were saying,
"Noah, build a boat.
There's only one requirement.
It only has to float."

We need this excellent lesson:
Like Noah and his "boat,"
For us to trust God's guiding,
We only have to float.

I Did This For You

I did this for you
When I came to earth,
Exchanging my Heavenly throne
For a lowly human birth.

My birth was in a stable
In a manger of hay.
Who'd have thought that your Savior
Would be born that way?

You couldn't save yourself
Because all have sinned.
I came to earth to save you
From the penalty of your sins.

I went to the cross--
All your sins to bear.
I bore them all for you
While I was dying there.

Your sins will be forgiven
If you believe in Me.
As I arose from death,
You will live eternally.

I love you very much
And want to be a part
Of everything you do.
Please invite me into your heart.

And please respect My birth
With love and adoration.
Please don't leave me out
Of your Christmas celebration.

Remember that My birth
Began what you couldn't do:
To free you from your sins.
I did this for <u>you</u>!

The Cross Gets Oh So Heavy, Lord.

The cross gets oh so heavy, Lord,
With trouble everywhere.
Enemies surround us, Lord.
We're tossed from here to there.

The cross gets oh so heavy, Lord,
As day after day goes by.
Sometimes the weight is so intense
We want to cry and cry.

The cross gets oh so heavy, Lord.
It feels as if we'll fall;
But we must trust You every day,
For You are Lord of all.

The cross gets oh so heavy, Lord.
Sometimes we feel despair;
But You said You won't send a cross
Heavier than we can bear.

But when our cross gets heavy, Lord,
Is when we need you the most.
We need to climb up on Your lap
And let You hold us close.

The cross gets oh so heavy, Lord.
We want to cry, "Why me?"
It's then that we need to remember
Your death upon that tree.

For You had the heaviest cross of all
When You bore the sins of the world
For the forgiveness of each one of us--
Each man, woman, boy and girl.

So, when our cross gets heavy, Lord,
Remind us that You bore OUR cross
So that each one who believes in You
Will live forever and not be lost.

What Do People Know?

I want to be a witness
To everyone I know,
To everyone I meet,
Everywhere I go.

I want them to know You, Jesus.
You live inside of me.
I want them to know what You are like
When they look at me.

But I just keep on stumbling
In my daily walk,
And I keep on failing
In my daily talk.

They know me when I'm angry.
They know me when I'm sad.
They know me when I'm selfish.
They know me when I'm bad.

But do they know You, Jesus?

They know me when impatient.
They know me when I wail.
They know me when I'm judging
Others when they fail.

But do they know You, Jesus?

Oh, Jesus, how I fail you
Many times a day,
In many things I do,
In many things I say,

In many things I think,
In things I fail to do,
In things I fail to say.
Oh, Lord, how I fail You.

For I'm to be a witness
Of You and all that's good.
Instead, I keep on doing
Things You never would.

For Your own life was perfect,
The way that mine should be.
You never gave into the sins
That keep on plaguing me.

Jesus, I want them to know,
When my sins are easy to see,
You disapprove, but You understand.
You forgive, and You keep loving me.

So one thing I hope they know,
When they come to know me,
Is that my sins are forgiven
Because You died on that tree.

You took my sins and theirs
And bore them on the cross
So we would be forgiven,
And we would not be lost.

The only thing You ask
Is that we would believe,
Then repent of all our sins
While to Your hand we cleave.

So, Lord, I'll keep on trying,
Although I'll trip and fall,
To become more and more like You--
The Perfect Example for all.

Then may they know You, Jesus.

Then may they know You love them,
Each as imperfect as I.
You loved us all so much that
You went to the cross to die.

You arose from the grave to show us
That You will always forgive;
And if, in You, we believe,
We, too, will forever live.

Praise God, we know You, Jesus!

You Don't Know What You're Missing

You don't know what you're missing--
Something that will not wait--
A beautiful sunrise that's happening
While you are sleeping late.

You don't know what you're missing
When you're busy all the day,
While a little child is begging
For you to come and play.

You don't know what you're missing
When you're hurriedly mowing your lawn--
Dandelions and wildflower blossoms
So pretty with dew from the dawn.

You don't know what you're missing
When Christmas is just Santa Claus,
With gifts, food and never a mention
Of Whose wonderful birth it was.

You don't know what you're missing
When Easter is full of strife,
Filling baskets with no mention
Of Who rose to Eternal Life.

You don't know what you're missing
When your life's filled with emptiness,
That Jesus can fill that void
If, to Him, you will just say yes.

So be sure that you will not be missing
Your chance to be free from sin,
For He's standing, knocking, and waiting
For you to invite Him in.

Be sure that you will not be missing
Having Him live in your heart,
And Eternal Life in Heaven where
Believing loved ones never part.

You Never Know When

You never know when
The tears will flow.
When you have lost loved ones,
You just never know.

You cry at first,
Then the tears subside.
You think that's the end
Of the tears you've cried.

But, as time goes by,
You realize
That tears will keep flowing
From your eyes.

You'll be alone
Driving along--
Finally happy,
Singing a song.

Suddenly, you'll see
A sight, and then
The tears will start flowing
Once again.

You'll be sitting in church
Feeling at peace,
Then the music will trigger
Tears that won't cease.

You'll be in a store
And smell a pie baking.
The memory brings tears,
And your heart starts aching.

The only real peace
That you can be given
Is they're not in those graves,
But they're living in Heaven.

That is because
In Christ they believed;
And that's why, for them,
You must not grieve.

To see them again,
Invite Christ in
To live in your heart
And forgive you of sin.

You never know when
Your own time will come,
When you'll take your last breath,
Your life on earth done.

You must decide now--
Ask Christ into your heart.
You'll live in Heaven where
Believing loved ones never part.

The Morning Star

They say it's always darkest
Just before the dawn.
The many stars that filled the sky
Suddenly are gone.

But just before the light of day
Begins to replace the night,
We look to the heavens, and there we see
One star so very bright.

The thousands of other stars
That were shining through the night
Have suddenly disappeared
As the sky started growing bright.

Though the stars cannot be seen,
We know that they're still there.
They're like our Lord, Whom we can't see,
But He's still everywhere.

The morning star reminds us
As we go from the darkness of night,
That God will never leave us--
He sent us that star so bright.

As we travel through the darkness
Before the light of day,
His single star reminds us
That He's there to light our way.

We'll never walk in darkness,
No matter where we are;
For Jesus said in His Bible,
"I am the bright Morning Star".

Who Would Do This For You?

Who would love you so very much
That, to save you, he'd give his life?
Would it be your loving husband?
Would it be your wife?

Who would possibly love you enough
To make that supreme sacrifice?
Who would ever love you enough
To pay that highest price?

Would it be your loving parents
Who brought you into this world?
Would it be your own dear child,
Your little boy or girl?

Would it be your dearest friend,
The one who loves you so,
Who'd give his very life for you;
Or would anyone you know?

Do you know there's One Who did this--
One Who gave His life for you?
Take time to think about it now.
Perhaps you never knew.

The One Who loved you so very much
Is Jesus, Who was willing to give
His very life for you on a cross,
Then arose from the grave and lives.

He took all your sins upon Himself,
He Who was without sin.
He'll forgive you and wash your sins away
If you will invite Him in.

Admit that you're sorry for your sins,
And ask Him your sins to forgive.
Thank Him for dying in your place
So, like Him, you'll forever live.

Please Accept This Gift

As young children, we love getting gifts.
We don't care one bit about giving.
But as we grow older, we learn
That to give adds much joy to our living.

Some people who just give and give
Are too proud to accept a gift.
They seem to forget that accepting
Provides the "giver's" spirit a lift.

The trouble we have accepting gifts
Is the reason we don't seem to "get it"--
That salvation is God's gift to us.
All we have to do is accept it!

We can't get it by living a good life.
We can't get it by doing a good deed.
We can't get it by trying to buy it.
We must acknowledge our spiritual need.

Salvation we do not deserve.
Salvation we can't earn or win.
We must ask Jesus our sins to forgive;
Open our hearts, and invite Him in.

If a billion-dollar gift is offered
In a check that's made out to you,
Until you reach out and accept it,
What good will it do for you?

Salvation is worth more than billions!
It's your future in eternity!
Will you spend it in the presence of your Savior
Or where you would not want to be?

To live on eternally in Heaven,
In Jesus we must believe.
Our salvation He freely gives us.
His gift we must freely receive.

Our sin debt was paid in full
When He died on the cross for each one.
He's knocking at the door of your heart.
Accept God's greatest gift, His Son.

The Tape Recording

How would we feel
If the things that we say
Were recorded for others
To hear every day?

If our voices were recorded,
Would we be proud
To have someone hear
Our thoughts spoken aloud?

Too often we're tempted
To slip into sin.
When speaking with someone,
We let Satan in.

We think what we say
Will only be heard
By those who are listening
To our spoken words.

So we let down our guard;
Say things that are mean;
Things that we'd never
Want heard or seen.

With all the recorders
Available out there,
Tape recorders and camcorders
Are now everywhere.

What if we were recorded?
What if we were caught
Saying embarrassing things--
Saying what we should not?

What we must remember
As we speak to listening ears:
They're not the only ones listening.
Our Lord in Heaven hears.

He hears all that we say.
He knows all that we do.
He knows all that we think.
What's he thinking of me and you?

But He's a loving God.
When we've made a mistake,
And ask for His forgiveness,
He completely erases the tape.

The Cross

When we wear crosses around our necks,
Made from silver or gold brightly gleaming,
Do we stop to ponder the actual cross
Or think about its meaning?

In churches the crosses are wooden or gold,
And they are polished and clean.
As we look at them, do we think at all
Or ponder what they mean?

The body of Jesus on a crucifix
Doesn't begin to show
The beating He accepted for you and for me
As He suffered blow after blow.

The beating was so long and so severe
He could hardly be identified--
Swelling and torn flesh all over His body
And a spear plunged deep in His side.

The cross upon which our Savior died
Was roughly hewn from wood.
When Jesus was taken down from the cross,
The empty cross still stood.

But that cross was not polished nor pleasant to see;
Neither was that cross clean.
For the cross that was standing was covered with blood,
And that is what the cross means.

The beating He took there should have been ours,
The crown of thorns on our head.
But He took our sins upon Himself
And chose to die in our stead.

From now on, whenever we look at a cross,
Let's remember how it was then.
Let's picture it covered with our own blood,
For our blood it should have been!

Let's thank our Savior for what He did,
For the forgiveness of our sins.
Let's be forever grateful to Christ--
Open our hearts and invite Him in.

Let's thank Him for giving us eternal life;
For after death, He has risen!
And because He lives, we, too, will live
With believing loved ones in Heaven.

Could You Do This?

Could you create a flower?
Could you create a tree?
Could you create a vegetable
Without planting any seeds?

Could you create a person,
A little girl or boy,
Where no other person existed--
No sperm and egg to join?

Could you create all animals
Each according to its kind--
None ever crossing species,
Only mating in his own line?

Could you create an earth?
Could you create a sky?
Could you create the fish
And all the birds that fly?

Could you create the nights?
Could you create the days?
Could you create the seasons
To be the same always?

Could you create the heavens
Filled with planets and stars,
Always in their same places
Like Jupiter and Mars?

Could you create the moon
To come out every night?
Could you create the sun
To give us daily light?

And, speaking of the sun,
Could you filter out its rays
So you won't be burned alive
Like you're in a microwave?

None of us can do this,
Not you, not I--no, none!
God alone is the answer.
He created everyone.

He created it all from nothing.
He created woman and man.
He created everything that IS,
According to His Plan.

Could you save yourself
From your sins that lead to death?
No one can save himself,
Only Jesus' atoning death.

That's why He sent you Jesus
To save you from your sins,
If you will just repent,
Open your heart and ask Him in.

The Blending of Our Families

Our lives were broken
And filled with pain.
We weren't at all sure
That we'd be happy again.

My two daughters and I
Were living alone
Trying to cope
In a broken home.

He was doing likewise,
With a daughter and son,
Trying alone
His family to run.

But God was watching
And honored our faith--
Allowed us to meet
And come face to face.

We fell in love,
Not only with each other,
But all of our children
Were like sisters and a brother.

We decided to marry
And start a new life,
And God truly blessed us
As husband and wife.

With Christ as the Head,
The way it should be,
We'll thank Him forever
For our blended family.

The Little Lost Sheep

Dear Lord, I'm so tired,
But I cannot sleep.
I am feeling like
The Biblical lost sheep.

I'm feeling as if
I am losing my way
In the things that I do
And the things that I say.

Life gets so hard
As we live day by day.
In times like these
It's easy to stray--

To stray from Your path,
To stray from You,
To say things and do things
That we shouldn't do.

I'm needing Your help
In my daily life,
In being a mother,
In being a wife,

In being a Christian
As I travel this sod,
In being an example
To lead others to You, Lord.

But I keep on stumbling
And too often fall,
Feeling discouraged
And wanting to bawl.

My greatest disappointment
Is when I fail You.
It's the worst thing in life!
It's not what I want to do!

But, Dear Lord, You find me
Like the little lost sheep,
Lift me up, hold me close
While I gratefully weep.

You hold me. You love me.
My sins You forgive.
Then You gently release me
To go on and live.

It's so comforting to know
That You're never far away
To gently guide me back
Whenever I stray.

This knowledge is wonderful!
I'm now feeling release
From the guilt I was bearing.
I'm now filled with Your peace.

I'm no longer feeling
Like the little lost sheep.
Reassured of Your forgiveness,
I can get back to sleep.

Thank You, Dear Lord.

Follow the Light

When I turn off the light
In the livingroom,
I can't see a thing
Except darkness and gloom.

I don't dare to move.
I even balk.
It's much too dark
To even walk.

Then suddenly I see
Three tiny lights.
On the VCR,
Three numbers are bright.

Then I realize
Which way to go.
Those illuminated numbers
My way will show.

When our lives get dark,
When things are tough,
When we trip and stumble
On a road that is rough,

We must follow Jesus,
The "Light of the World."
He'll lead us safely through
All the trials of this world.

Then, if we follow Him,
Through our earthly strife,
He'll lead us through death
Into Eternal Life.

A Hole in Your Sole

Oh no, your shoe
Has developed a hole
In the worst place.
It's in the sole.

A hole in your sole
Lets pebbles in
That hurt your foot
And pierce your skin.

A hole in your sole
Lets mud in
That wets your foot
And soils your skin.

A hole in your sole
Makes your act
Very agitated
When you step on a tack.

Who can repair
The hole in your sole?
Only a cobbler
Can fill that hole.

Oh, what comfort
It brings to you.
When your sole is repaired,
You walk anew.

The same is true
Of the hole in your <u>soul</u>.
Everything's wrong
Till it's made whole.

Life is annoying
From morning to night--
Only aggravations
Till it's made right.

Who can repair
The hole in your soul?
Only Jesus Christ
Can fill that hole.

After Jesus
Has filled that hole,
You're filled with peace,
And you're finally whole.

I'm Feeling Complete

Last night when I got into bed
And I began to pray,
I couldn't stop thanking God because
I'd had such a wonderful day.

Our family had all come together
To honor Christ Jesus' birth
At our Christmas celebration
Of the day He came to earth.

Our own three children were here,
Each with their own spouse,
With eight grandchildren as well
Who really enlivened our house!

When my husband and I sat down to eat
With our children, spouses, girls and boys,
I said, "This does my heart good."
My heart overflowed with joy!

The day was filled with fun
And lots of noise and motion.
At the end of the day when I prayed,
My prayer was filled with emotion.

I thanked God over and over.
The memories of the day were sweet.
I said, "Thank you, Lord, for my family.
Right now, I'm feeling complete."

When the children are grown and scattered,
They seldom all come the same day.
It happens only once or twice a year,
And then they each go their own way.

So, I was feeling once more complete
Like a bird with her chicks 'neath her wings.
If only I could hold them once more
Like when babies, my heart would sing.

For their families and my dear children,
Whom I can no longer hold,
I'll never be forever complete
Till they are all "in the fold".

That's how it must be with the Lord
When we, His children have strayed
Away from Him much too far
And continue to stay away.

He longs for us to come home.
He wants that more than anything.
He is filled with the ultimate joy
When He gathers us under His wings.

Faith in the Unseen

Today we saw an example,
With the help of a kind, young man,
Of an act that showed faith at work
In a way we could understand.

I had taken my car for repair
In his shop with an entrance that's small.
To back the car out when finished,
It's quite close to a cement wall.

When backing out of the shop
Through the driveway that's somewhat tight,
To turn the car around and drive away,
You have to cut the wheels to the right.

Because my car is a van,
It's difficult to see out the rear;
And up front, I can't see the hood,
So I couldn't tell when the wall was near.

I was about to drive the car forward,
Then back out like other times before
By making the necessary corrections;
But the young man was coming out of the door.

He had noticed my concern,
So he approached the car on my side.
He directed me while I backed up,
And he became my guide.

I thanked him and then I said,
"That's how it is with faith.
You must believe in the unseen."
He agreed with a smile on his face.

The "unseen" was not seeing out the back
Nor the front which was close to the wall;
But this young man became my guide,
And I trusted him through it all.

That's how it is with Jesus.
He will always be by our side
If we put our faith in Him.
Through the unseen, He'll be our Guide.

The Season of Spring is New Life

After a long, cold winter
Filled with tons of snow,
We can hardly wait for spring
And the brightness of its glow.

Each day new beauty surrounds us
Helping to rid us of strife
As winter's dull colors disappear
And all nature springs back to life.

The birds come back to our region
With their lovely uplifting songs.
It's so good to have them return
After being gone all winter long.

We wait for tiny green shoots
To poke up through the melting snow
With their buds which soon will follow
Bursting forth with a colorful glow.

We continue to notice more colors
Appearing in our yard every day
And wild flowers of every hue
On our path along the way.

Bright flowering buds appear
On the trees that all winter were bare.
They also show bright colors
As we look around everywhere.

Sadly, not everyone appreciates
These God-created flowers on their lawn.
They're not content till their lawn is just
      green
And all the colored flowers are gone.

But for those of us who appreciate
Every God-given gift,
The new life of spring is wonderful.
It gives our spirit a lift.

That's how it is when we invite Jesus
Into our heart, and we're born anew.
The joy in our heart springs forth
With beauty that's fresh and new.

Our lives are just like winter.
They are dark and don't mean a thing.
But when Jesus comes into our heart,
He gives us new life like spring.

And then, because He arose
After dying on the cross,
We, too, will live on in Heaven
Eternally and not be lost.

Cock A Doodle Doo

"Hey, Everybody,
I'm a real cool cock!
The only rooster,
I'm the head of the flock.

"We were hangin' out
In the coop the other day,
Waitin' for the eggs
That the hens would lay.

"I was struttin'
Around for the dames,
When all of a sudden,
We saw some flames.

"We all got quiet.
You couldn't hear a sound.
Then we all started squawkin'
And runnin' around.

"All of a sudden,
We saw a hand
Reachin' through the smoke.
It sure looked grand.

"This firefighter
Was a guy named Jeff.
He grabbed us all
Till no one was left.

"He'd grab a wing.
He'd grab a leg.
He wouldn't let go,
No matter how we'd beg.

"He'd pass us out
To some dudes in a line
Who'd pass us to our owner.
It sure worked out fine.

"But with our friend, the duck,
They couldn't win.
He kept gettin' rescued
But would waddle back in.

"This guy finally grabbed him
And held on tight.
He was rescued once more,
So now he's all right.

"We lost a few hens;
And, for that, we're real sad.
But, for this guy, Jeff,
We are really glad.

"He pulled us out
Without any fear.
I can see why he won
"Firefighter of the Year".

"I heard he's a Christian;
So me and the dames
Will thank his God
For savin' us from the flames.

"And to all of those dudes,
We apologize
For the smells on their clothes
When they got home that night.

"They'd washed all their gear
At the station that night;
But, when they got home,
They still didn't smell right.

"I've heard that Marcia,
This Jeff-dude's wife,
Said, 'That's a smell I hope to never
Smell again in my life!'"

Our Savior

My husband and I
Down a long, steep hill drove
To find our friend's house
On a snow-covered camp road.

But this was not
The road of our friend.
At the bottom of the hill
It looked like a dead end.

When we turned around
And began to drive
Up the slippery hill,
We started to slide.

We backed the car
All the way down the hill,
Tried to drive up again;
But it was all for nil.

There was a layer of ice
Beneath the packed snow.
No matter how we tried,
Up the hill we couldn't go.

We backed down and tried
Six or seven more times;
But always, halfway up
Was the most we could climb.

We were not even sure
That a towing truck
Could climb the icy hill.
We'd both have been stuck.

We were getting concerned
About what to do.
Every camp looked deserted,
So we thought no one knew.

At the bottom of the hill
Three roads looked like dead ends,
So we didn't know how
This crisis would end.
We kept outwardly calm,
But I silently prayed
For God to help us
Get out of that place.

When we were about
To give it all up,
At the bottom of the hill
Appeared a man with his pup.

He jokingly said,
"I could watch you all day!
You're really persistent!"
He then made our day.

What he told us meant
We wouldn't need to be towed
If we'd turn to the left
And drive out his road.

There would be no hill
If we went that way.
Those words were so welcome
That I had to say:

"You are the answer
To my prayers."
He laughed and we talked.
Then he left us there.

We drove out that road
With a great sigh.
What would we have done
If he hadn't come by?

We had both thought
There was no way to go,
But this man saved us
When the right way he showed.

That's how it is
With our Savior, our Lord.
He guides us through
The times when we're lost.

If we will just
In Him put our faith,
He will save us;
And we'll live in His grace.

Because our Lord Jesus,
Went to the cross,
Our sins He'll forgive.
We'll no longer be lost!

Created Creatures

This morning I was watching
Little birds eating seeds
Right outside our front door,
Fulfilling their hunger needs.

One of them was a sparrow.
One was a chickadee.
Each was easily recognized
As the kind of bird it would be.

Exactly as God created them,
They continue to look the same:
Each tiny feather in place
So we can call them by name.

The same was true of animals
Till humans did what they do:
Cross-breeding cocker spaniels and poodles,
Thus creating a cockapoo.

When God created those birds,
It was part of His Master Plan,
Every feather forming a pattern
Easily identified by man.

When God created humans,
In His image, He created us,
Every finger and toe in place
Since He created Adam from dust.

He has numbered each hair on our head.
He knows each of us by name.
Each one of us is unique.
None of us is the same.

The markings on birds are not random.
They're all beautiful and precise.
They're all a part of God's plan
So each bird can be recognized.

The same must be true of how Christians
Should be recognized everywhere:
By the way that we look and live
And by the fruit that we bear.

The Storms of Life

When I awoke and looked out
Our bedroom window this morning,
I could barely see the trees
As the day was slowly dawning.

But I could see enough
To know that the storm had passed
Because I could see the birches
Standing still at last.

Yesterday and last night
All of the birches in the yard
Were tossing back and forth
While the wind blew very hard.

The calm of the birches this morning
Reminds me of the storms of life.
Sometimes we're tossed and turned
With trouble and with strife.

Then as the day grew brighter,
I could see other birches bent low,
Trapped forever beneath other trees
From an ice storm two years ago.

Some people bounce back from trouble
And find peace of mind to stand tall.
Some are crippled and find themselves
Trapped forever beneath it all.

True peace comes from Jesus, our Savior.
He's the calm in the midst of the storm.
His grace, His forgiveness, His love
Gives us peace and strength to go on.

A Very Tough Day

There's a little bed empty
Tonight in his town,
For today a four-year-old
Little boy drowned.

When the family was at
The river today,
He slipped into the water
And was swept away.

He was finally found,
But it was too late.
Attempts to revive him
Were not his fate.

He was taken to Heaven
On angels' wings.
He is now happy there
While Heaven sings.

He'll be there to welcome
His loved ones someday
When it is their time
To pass away.

Till then, he'll hope his loved ones
Will believe in God
And will accept Jesus
As their Savior and Lord.

That's what they must do,
And happily he'll wait,
Till they'll all be together
Inside Heaven's gate.

Reaching for the Sun

Today I drove past tiger lilies.
The whole group of flowers looked like one,
For all of these bright orange flowers
Were reaching toward the sun.

Their reaching looked so unnatural--
The whole group was stretching and leaning,
Reaching toward their nourishment
Which down from the sun was beaming.

These flowers seem to know what is needed
In order for them to grow.
They all know in which direction
Each of them has to go.

These flowers seem smarter than we are.
They know what to do to survive.
They know they must reach toward the sun
In order to stay alive.

Instinctively each of these flowers
Reaches out for its life from the sun.
Why can't we humans do likewise
And reach for new life through God's Son?

Salvation comes from believing in Jesus.
Through His forgiveness, He sets us free;
And because He died to save us,
In Heaven we'll live eternally!

Thank You, Father

Thank You, Father, for this morning.
Thank You for this day that's dawning.
Thank You for the sun that's rising.
Thank You for clouds on the horizon.

People will wonder, this I know,
Why I thank You for clouds here below.
I will tell them the reason why
There's not as much beauty in a cloudless sky:

When the sun is shining with no clouds nearby,
Only the color blue meets your eyes.
When the sun is shining on clouds here below,
Red, pink and orange colors glow.

Thank You, Father, for the trees
Gently swaying in the breeze.
Thank You for the fresh, white snow
Covering the ground down here below.

Thank You for the pink color that's peeping.
Over the horizon, that pink is now creeping
Coloring all of those gray clouds pink.
It's so beautiful! I can hardly think!

I must watch it closely, this I know,
For the colors will fade very quickly and go.
In fact, while I was having my say,
The pink clouds have now turned back to gray.

The gray clouds are moving quickly, I think.
New clouds above the sun are now turning pink.
Thank You, Father, for the beauty I see.
Thank You for sharing Your blessings with me.

Thank You, Father, for this time with You.
Thank You for helping in all that I do.
Thank You for the talent that You've given me
To share in rhyme Your blessings I see.

The Message

Dear Lord, I was so discouraged
Last night when I got into bed.
Sorrowful thoughts from the day
Still swirled around in my head.

I couldn't get to sleep.
The tears continued to flow.
Inside me, a storm was raging.
Out-of-doors, howling winds did blow.

I needed to talk to You.
Needing hope, I started to pray.
I said only, "Dear Lord" and opened my eyes;
And Your message came right away!

The only lights in the room
Were red numbers on the clock.
What they showed just stunned me--
It was such a total shock!

The numbers displaying the time
Were "3:16" in the morn.
My darkened mood immediately left,
And then those numbers moved on.

I know that it was a message
Sent to me straight from You:
The most important "John 3:16"
Telling us what we must do:

> "For God so loved the world,
> that He gave His only begotten Son,
> that whosoever believeth in Him
> should not perish, but have
> everlasting life."

Dear Lord, thank You for this verse,
A definite message from You.
It took my focus off myself
And put it back on You.

They'll Be Alone

This is the toughest
Poem I'll ever write.
I've been awake grieving
Nearly all night.

They made it clear
That they don't believe;
And now, for them,
We can only grieve.

For them there's no meaning
On Christmas Day
When loved ones gather
And celebrate.

Christians gather together
On Christmas morn
Exchanging gifts
Because Jesus was born.

For them, there's no meaning
When they celebrate
On Easter Sunday
With each filled plate.

Christians celebrate Easter
Because each one knows:
Death couldn't hold Jesus
And He arose!

They'll be alone
By a loved one's bed
With no hope at all
When their loved one is dead.

They'll be alone
With the choice they've made:
Lonely and empty,
Deserted and afraid.

They'll be alone
While those they loved
Are safe with Jesus
In Heaven above.

They'll be alone
When they take their last breath
Walking through the Valley
Of the Shadow of Death.

I hate to say this,
But I'll say it again:
When they denounce Jesus,
It's over for them.

There are only two choices:
Heaven or Hell.
The choice is theirs
Where forever they'll dwell.

But, praise God for Christmas:
Our Savior was born.
When they ask His forgiveness,
In Heaven, They'll live on.

Our Daddy

Today I saw a daddy
Standing in a crowd.
Everyone was screaming--
Shouting very loud.

They had all been waiting
To hear a person sing,
But the daddy's little girl
Couldn't see a thing.

She was standing next to him--
Could not be seen at all.
When her daddy picked her up,
She then looked very tall.

It was only then
That she could look around
And see all she hadn't seen
While standing on the ground.

That's how it is with us--
Sometimes we cannot see
What's happening around us.
We're frightened as can be.

But then, our Father, God,
Reaches down His Hands
And gently lifts us up.
Then everything is grand.

We can always cling to Him
Whenever times get rough,
Knowing He's our Father
        To help when things are tough.

He's always there for us
In good times and in bad.
He is our greatest blessing--
The best we'll ever have.

Unto Us A Child Was Born

This year on February 21,
A day that was divine,
Our family welcomed a baby:
Grandchild number nine!

Abigail fills our lives
With joy all the while
And warms all of our hearts
With her precious smile.

I try to spend as much time
With her as I can do
Because I am well aware
That I'm now seventy-two.

Her birth is a reminder,
And I sometimes shed a tear:
When she turns twenty-one,
I may not be here.

Of course, I do not know
How long my life will be;
But my parents lived to
Ninety-two and ninety-three.

Only our Lord knows
How long I can stay
On earth with my dear ones
Loving them every day.

The greatest wish I have
For everyone that I love
Is to spend eternity
With them in Heaven above.

This causes me to pause
And wonder about you:
Won't you want to be with
All your loved ones too?

Well, unto ALL was born
Our Saviour, Jesus Christ.
The only way to be saved
Is to ask Him into our life.

If we repent of our sins,
Jesus will forgive;
And, in Heaven with our loved ones,
We will forever live.

God's Cable

This morning I was watching
A news segment on TV.
The story being told was
About a huge concrete beam.

The measurement of the beam
Was the largest of its kind.
It was one hundred feet long,
Five inches deep, six feet wide.

The beam was being hoisted
Up by a very large crane,
Moving it high to place it
On a waiting truck here in Maine.

A man was standing below it
Beside the waiting truck
Which would then transport it
To its destination with luck.

As the beam was being lowered,
It twisted sideward on the crane.
The man reached up his hands
And straightened it as it came.

This was amazing to me:
Watching the man who was able
To move this beam without effort
As it hung there on the cable.

This scene was a lesson to me,
And hopefully to others as well.
We can't do everything alone,
So this story I wanted to tell.

When things are too heavy for us,
We must place them into God's "cable".
He will help us do the impossible:
Things of which we're not able.

We can't move a huge beam alone.
It's impossible for us to do;
But, "With God, all things are possible."
He'll help us to carry it through.

Where Are You?

Where are you
Since you've gone from me?
You, in person,
I no longer see.

I wander around
And feel so alone
When I realize
You're not coming home.

Half of me is missing
Since you have gone
Because God had joined us
Into one.

Non-believers would say
That you're in the grave;
But you believed in Jesus,
So you were "saved".

Saved from death
Because Jesus died.
Now you are walking
By His side.

The greatest peace
That I can be given
Is that you did not die,
But are living in Heaven.

I believe in Jesus
And look forward to when
You and I will be
Together again.

But until then,
What will I do
When I'm hurting so much
From missing you?

I'll ask myself,
"What would you want for
      me?",
I know you wouldn't want

Me overcome by grief.
I'll thank God for
The time that we had--
All of the good times
And the bad.

I'll thank Him for
Our children who blessed
Our lives with such love
And happiness.

I'll thank Him for
Our grandchildren, too,
Who brought so much joy
To me and you.

I'll thank Him for
My memories.
In them you're always
Here with me.

I'll thank Him that
Memories will keep you a part
Of me, for you'll always
Be in my heart.

I'll thank Him that
Memory will allow me to feel
Your arms around me
When I'm needing to heal.

I'll thank Him most of all
For your belief,
And that will help me
Not to grieve.

I'll thank Him that
I, too, believe;
And because He died,
In Heaven I'll be.

Until that time,
What will I do
To help me when
I'm missing you?

When I am stronger
And feel less pain,
I must try to start
To live again.

I'll try to find
Someone in need
Of comfort, and help him
As others helped me.

For that's what the Bible
Says to us--
We must comfort others
As God comforted us;

For then our suffering
Will not be in vain,
And we will begin
To heal again.

So, now that I know
Right where you are,
I'll continue to hold you
Close in my heart.

I'll continue to hold you
Close in memory
Until we're together
In Eternity.

And I'll pray for comfort
When I feel so alone,
Knowing God will care for me
Till He calls me Home.

The Flicker

Today my husband was standing
In front of the kitchen sink,
Drawing water from the faucet,
About to take a drink.

Suddenly something hit the window
With a thud which was very loud.
Startled, he looked up and saw a large bird
Falling away to the ground.

I was working in the living room
And also heard the loud thud.
I expected that, whatever hit the window,
Would be on the ground covered with blood.

We rushed to the window and saw
A flicker in a heap on the ground
About six feet away from the house.
He was lying there upside down.

We both felt sure he was dead,
But he finally managed to turn over.
He then raised his head way up
As he sat there among the clover.

For about ten minutes he sat there
With his head raised way up high.
Nothing was moving but his eyes
While his beak pointed up to the sky.

It was as if his instinct told him
That, in time his help would come,
If he sat very still and waited
And continued to look up above.

I was watching and praying,
"Dear Lord, as it says in that hymn,
'Your eye is on the sparrow.'
Now I pray that you'll watch over him."

Suddenly, the flicker moved
And hopped his usual three hops!
He paused and then hopped three more
    times.
Then around the corner, he hopped.

I ran through the house and looked out
To try to see where he had gone,
But he must have flown away.
He was nowhere on the lawn.

I smiled and sent up a prayer
And said, "I thank you, God.
You watch over birds. You watch over us.
You're our Savior and our Lord."

To me, this was a good lesson:
In times of trouble, we must wait
Quietly until our strength returns,
Always looking above with faith.

The Skids of Life

Yesterday I was driving
Down a very winding road.
I had just prayed for safety
And was in a traveling mode.

In an instant my car was skidding
Back and forth on a patch of ice.
I did all I could to stop it.
My heart was filled with fright.

Thankfully no cars were coming
While I was there in such need
Because this was on a curve,
And we would have collided indeed.

I was doing all I could do
As the car skidded to and fro.
Turning the car and applying the brakes,
I kept saying, "Oh no! Oh no!"

On the fifth skid, I said "Dear God".
In that instant the car was controlled!
There was no more skidding.
I traveled safely along the road.

Why do we wait so long?
Why do we struggle in fear?
Why don't we call on God sooner,
Knowing He's always near?

I know that this was a lesson
That the Lord was sending to me.
It's why I record it here
For everyone else to see.

On May 24, 1998, Priscilla Elliott asked me to write a new Firefighters' Prayer. They had just attended a funeral on May 18, 1998, in Kennebunk, ME, for George E. Lawrence. She didn't like the prayer that had been used, so she asked me to write a new one. I told her I would pray about it and try to write one. I did pray about it. I then kept waiting for God to answer because I had absolutely no idea what to write. How could I relate to being a firefighter and write a prayer for him to say?

I was still waiting for an answer to my prayer when, today, in Nashua, NH, I was driving along. A fire engine came speeding out of a side road with its siren screaming. All of the traffic pulled over to the side of the road to let the fire engine pass, and the poem immediately began to flow through me. It was as though I were there in the fire station hearing the alarm. My heart actually started racing like a firefighter's heart must race. I could then visualize myself on the fire engine speeding to the fire. I fumbled around in my pocketbook to find a piece of paper to write down the verses I was being given before I forgot them. I grabbed my checkbook and a pen and began to write on the deposit slips in the back of the checkbook. I was resting my checkbook on the top of the steering wheel and the horn in the middle of it. While driving through fairly heavy traffic on Route 3 in Nashua, I was writing. From time to time, the weight of my hands on the checkbook would beep the horn! (By the way, I was keeping my eyes on the road and not looking at what I was writing, which is evident by looking at my nearly illegible handwriting on the back of the first two deposit slips!)

When I was nearly home and about to exit Route 3 in Billerica, MA, the last two verses were coming. I knew I couldn't go home right then because I would start speaking with my husband and would lose the verses from my mind; so, I turned onto the street which Dutile School is on, stopped the truck, and finished writing the last two verses of the poem on the back of the third deposit slip.

<u>When A Firefighter Hears the Alarm</u>

When the alarm sounds,
My heart starts to race.
I know not what
I'm about to face.

And so, Dear Lord,
I pray once more,
As I always pray,
That You'll go before.

I pray that You
Will protect and shield
Us all from harm.
To You, I yield.

Guide us all.
Bring us through
All that You would
Have us do.

If my earthly body
I must leave,
You know that, in Jesus,
I believe.

We all must believe,
Ask Him into our heart.
In eternal life
We'll never part.

When Your alarm sounds
For my life to cease,
I know that I shall
Go in peace.

For I will see
My Savior there.
With believing loved ones,
Eternity I'll share.

FAMILY

Our minister, Jim Key, at the First Baptist Church of Shapleigh, Maine, had given us an assignment the previous Sunday, to bring something to church to share who we were with the congregation. Carpenters would bring in a hammer; fishermen would bring in a fishing pole; etc. As the day approached, this poem was forming in my mind. On January 23, 1990, I was awakened by God's nudging. I started the poem at 3 a.m. and finished it at 3:16 a.m. Still being shy about my poems, I took it to church with me, but never got up my nerve to share it!

My Life's Goal

What is it that
I want to be?
A good example
For all to see.

To be a good Christian
Is what I want most.
Living in God's grace
So that I may not boast.

Accepting His love,
Forgiveness, and peace.
In times of trouble,
It will not cease.

Remembering not
To do or to say
Anything to lead
One person astray.

A good daughter to my parents
I hope I have been.
They've given me so much
And would give it again.

A good wife to my husband
I'll try to be,
Because he has always been
So good to me.

A good mother to my children,
I'll try to be the kind
Of example for them
To follow behind.

A good grandmother to my
Grandchildren and then,
Hopefully I'll be an
Inspiration to them.

A good friend to the people
I meet on the way,
Until we're together
In Heaven, I pray.

I wrote this poem about our granddaughter on my husband, Ernie's, birthday, which was on April 30, 1994. Bonnie Newell, was at the time, six years old, the daughter of our daughter, Marcia and her husband, Jeff. She was spending the day with us at our home in Massachusetts. She didn't want to go into our playhouse to play because "there might be spiders in there." I worked all day to clean it out for her. That night, memories began flooding in, and I wrote the following poem.

Playhouse

I cleaned up our little old playhouse today, put the furniture on the lawn.
She'd said, "I don't want to go in there and play until all the spiders are gone."

So I vacuumed the ceiling, the walls, and the door. I cleaned everything that I could.
I then washed and waxed the old well-worn floor, and
worked till the playhouse looked good.

Then, as I lovingly cleaned every piece of furniture out on the lawn,
The memories continued and would not cease of the times that forever were gone.

My own three dear children, each one with a friend, had spent so much time in there
Playing "pretend" games I thought wouldn't end, at the tiny table and chair.

Inviting their Mom and their Dad in for "tea" and "pouring" it out with such pride,
Showing us just how much fun it could be to be with them there inside.

The little piano that once used to play many a "pretend" little song,
That once got pounded a few times each day, has now sat silent too long.

The little old iron on the pink ironing board hasn't "ironed" a thing in years.
The little pink cradle and doll looking bored is enough to bring me to tears.

Over on the table, the shiny red phone does nothing but silently wait
To answer and say, "Nobody's home, a fact that I really hate."

The tiny refrigerator, tiny stove and sink, no longer shine, but are rusty.
The curtains, as well, need replacing, I think. And the "dress up" clothes are all musty.

My children who played in this playhouse have grown,
as all children must grow and depart.
Each of them now has a home of his own but will always be here in my heart.

And now God has sent her, for He is so good, our little granddaughter to share,
To play in our playhouse, if only I would, "Get rid of those spiders in there!"

In May of 1994, my husband, Ernie, and I had taken his mother, Mary Johnson, to visit her daughter, Patricia Parker in Denver, Colorado. One day Patricia drove us to Boulder. Her mother was riding in the passenger side of the front seat, and Ernie and I were in the back. While we were driving there, Patricia stopped the car, facing the beautiful Rocky Mountain range in the distance. She told us that "America The Beautiful" was written in approximately that same spot. She took her mother's hand and began singing the song softly. It was a beautiful scene both in the front seat and beyond to the mountains. That night I was inspired to write this poem.

A Colorado Memory

"O beautiful for spacious skies,
For amber waves of grain,"
Love shining from Patricia's eyes
As she starts to explain:

Katherine Lee Bates was inspired here
To write that lovely song.
The reason why becomes quite clear
The more we drive along.

With mother seated by her side,
Patricia starts to sing,
Softly, sweetly, as we ride,
In awe of everything.

"For purple mountain majesties".
We're riding right along
Toward those mountains joyously
While Patricia sings the song.

We're in awe of being there,
And we can plainly see
The reason that this is where
That great song came to be.

This memory I shall always keep
Of those two hand in hand,
Patricia singing soft and sweet
About God's glorious land.

Now every time I hear that song,
I once again am there,
Hearing her sing as we ride along....
This memory we'll always share.

This somewhat silly little poem was written at 5:45 a.m. on December 11, 1994, while thinking about my two daughters, Marcia, age 29, and Christine, age 22, and their closeness as sisters and how it has increased through the years.

My Sister

When I was little
And she was big,
I kissed her
    My sister.

As I grew older,
I always tried
To "assist" her
    My sister.

When my foot hurt,
She put a BandAid on
My blister
    My sister.

She'd play with me
When I wanted to
Play Twister
    My sister.

I'd have taken her side
If anyone had
Booed or hissed her
    My sister.

Then a boy came along,
And he could not
Resist her
    My sister.

It became quite clear
That he would become
The "Mister," to
    My sister.

When they got married
And moved away,
How I missed her
    My sister.

Now I'm married, too.
I thank God that
He blessed us
    As sisters.

Please Don't Forget About Me

For years I filled your hearts with love,
With laughter, joy and glee.
Now that the new baby has arrived,
Please don't forget about me.

Remember that I once was small
And cute and cuddly,
But now that I am growing tall,
Please don't forget about me.

The baby takes up all the time
You used to have for me.
It seems that I can't even climb
Upon your loving knee.

I can still remember when
You thought I was cute and sweet,
But I am cranky now and then
Because you're forgetting me.

I never used to have to share
It's really hard to do.
For me, in the past, you were always there.
I'm really missing you.

When I am acting really bad
And naughty as can be,
Perhaps it's 'cause I'm feeling sad
And lonely, don't you see?

So give me lots of extra love
And all the hugs I need.
Please notice when I'm not getting enough.
Don't make me beg and plead.

Remember that our Lord above
Loves all of us equally.
Please be like Him when you give love,
And you won't forget about me!

This poem was written in December of 1995, after my husband's mother, Mary Johnson, had gone to be with the Lord in July of that year. Each year before Christmas, Ernie's sister, Patricia Johnson Parker Fiske, sends each of Mary's children and grandchildren a completely updated list of our Johnson family names, birth dates, addresses, phone numbers, and email addresses. That year of 1995 I felt moved to write a poem which would be comforting to the family members and have it included with the annual family list. I heard the verse of scripture, Psalm 147: 4, He counts the stars and calls them all by name, from the Living Bible; and it reminded me of Mary because, of the more that one hundred people on her family list, she knew them all by name. Although it was not included with the family list that year, I put copies of it in the "Johnson Family Memories" books that I gave to each of Mary's children in 2005.

The Johnson Family List

When our Family List was started
Several years ago,
None of us could realize
How quickly it would grow.

People were getting married.
Many babies were born.
Other names were added.
The list goes on and on.

No matter how many pages,
Nor how long the list became,
Grammie Johnson loved us all
And knew us all by name.

Each time a little baby's name
Was added to the list,
She knew exactly who it was
Not a single one was missed.

So, Little Ones, as you grow up,
Please remember this:
In Grammie's heart you were much more
Than a name on her Family List.

As does her Lord and Savior,
Whom she's with now above,
She thought we all were special
And gave us equal love.

This poem came to me at 10:30 p.m. on July 4, 1996, after thinking about a man to whom I was talking that morning at the Potting Shed restaurant. He had told me about how his brothers and sisters were fighting over inheritance. I suddenly felt more fortunate to have been an only child after all of the years of wishing I had brothers and sisters.

An Only Child

For years I mourned and longed to have
A sister or a brother.
I was their child and always felt that
There should be another.

Another child to spend time with,
To laugh and play all day.
But as the years went passing by,
None other came our way.

As I grew older and looked around,
I then began to see
The many things that I would miss
If there were more than me.

Their laps were mine; their love was mine;
They didn't have to share
Their time with any other child. For me,
They were always there.

I didn't have to fuss and fight
In sibling rivalry.
My friends and I were very close,
Like sisters and brothers should be.

I used to fear that my parents would die
And I would be alone.
I felt that way for many years,
In fact, till I was grown.

And now that I am all grown up,
Three children of my own,
And husband dear, and Jesus here,
I'll never be alone.

There's always been a vacant spot
A sibling would have filled,
But life is full and I'm so blessed
According to God's will.

And God has promised Eternal Life
If in Jesus we believe.
We all will be together one day.
Our loved ones, we'll never leave.

Our friends from Billerica, Massachusetts, Harold (Phip) and Jackie Phippen had a camp near us on Square Pond in Shapleigh, Maine. We had a dog named Tara, and they had a dog named Brownie. The Phippens and we were friends; their children and our children were friends; and their dog and ours became friends, as well. Our dog, Tara, died in August of 1988. Brownie died two years later in June of 1990. After learning of his death, I wrote the following poem about our two "doggie friends" and sent it to them.

Tara and Brownie

Tara and Brownie, our two doggie friends.
They met in Maine where the summers we spend.

They liked each other right from the start.
They'd play with each other until time to part.

When left alone, Tara'd go along
To Brownie's house and sing a sad song!

They got sprayed by skunks on different days
Which didn't please us, needless to say!

On rainy days, Brownie'd fall with a thud
To let her mistress clean off the mud!

There never were two more loyal pets
To their families who love them yet.

Our faithful friends are now both gone.
But in our memories, they will live on.

If there's a place in Heaven for dogs to stay,
I know Tara and Brownie will continue to play.

This poem was written on June 18, 1995. It was inspired by looking at our answering machine each time we come home and realizing that we are happy when we receive messages and disappointed when there are none.

The Answering Machine

The first thing I do
When I come home each day,
Is find out who called us
While we were away.

This answering machine
Is quite an invention.
Our loved ones can use it
To get our attention.

Our answering machine
Has a little red light
That blinks on and off
With its color so bright.

If the light blinks but once,
We've had but one call.
If the light's blinking twice,
Then two people called.

While gone a few days,
The blinks numbered nine.
We answered those calls
And thought it was fine!

But I must admit,
When we've come home and had
No blinking red light,
It made me feel sad.

I realize now
What our dear Lord must say
While He longs to hear from us
Day after day.

It must give him pleasure
When our "light is blinking".
When we talk with Him,
He's happy, I'm thinking

When our loved ones called us
And we were not here,
They must have been sad,
A recording to hear.

But when we call God,
The answer's rewarding,
For he's always there
We'll get no recording!

The Voice of a Child

Before the Easter Cantata, little Bethany
Was just as sweet as she could be.
She was drinking some milk while on Daddy's lap,
Not at all interested in taking a nap.

She started getting restless--a little bit bored.
She tried to relax but never did snore.
Her mom then decided to give her a book
To keep her amused while she gave it a look.

The music began and was really loud!
Bethany was startled along with the crowd!
She sat right up straight and started to look,
No longer interested in "reading" her book!

She stared intently at the action up there
To see what was happening everywhere.
Then, when the choir began singing their song,
Bethany joined them and sang right along!

Her baby voice just sounded so sweet.
She even managed to follow the beat!
Whenever they sang, she stopped everything,
And felt compelled to join in and sing!

She never made noise when they were just walking,
When a solo was sung, or they were just talking;
But, anytime that the whole choir sang,
Bethany's sweet baby-"alto" voice rang!

For us, it was something we'll never forget.
It was just about the sweetest thing yet!
Of the many voices--some of the best--
I think God heard Bethany's above all the rest!

"Walk in Grandpa's Footprints"

Today, I picked up our grandson,
Three-year-old Daniel, to take
Him for a ride to our camp
For a day of ice fishing on the lake.

Daniel's mother, our daughter, Christine,
Had him well prepared for the day--
All bundled up in warm clothes.
We were ready to go on our way.

He thought the ride was long,
As he sat buckled into his seat.
He could hardly move at all--
Just roll his eyes and move his feet!

Much earlier in the day,
His Grandpa Johnson had gone
To the camp to get the stove going
On that very cold, 12-degree morn.

When we arrived at the lake,
I brought the car to a stop
At the beginning of our long, steep driveway.
We had to park at the top.

My hands were full of bundles
Of things we would need for the day,
So I couldn't hold Daniel's hand
As we started on our way.

On the hill were patches of ice
As Daniel went on ahead.
It really made me concerned
That he'd fall and hurt his head.

Then I noticed his grandpa's footprints
Where he'd avoided the patches of ice.
I said, "Walk in Grandpa's footprints,"
And he followed my advice.

Then, when the day was ending,
Up the long hill we started to climb.
The ice patches were harder to see,
So I said the same thing one more time.

"Walk in your grandpa's footprints,"
Is good advice for a child every day
If his grandpa walks in Jesus' footprints;
For Jesus is The Truth, Life, and Way.

A Lesson I Wish I Had Learned

A little boy that I love
Learned a lesson today--
A lesson that I wish I
Had learned at his age.

Oh, what a difference
This lesson would have made
If, as a child, I'd learned
What I hope he learned today.

Today, in a moment of
Frustration of the day,
He said something that his parents
Didn't want him to say.

They took him aside,
While he started to pout,
Had a lengthy discussion
And gave him a "time out".

They then told him that
He must apologize.
He finally got through it
With tears in his eyes.

My heart was sorely aching
For what he was going through.
I just wanted to tell him,
"It's okay. I love you."

When he had finished,
I held him in my arms.
I wanted him to know
That he'd done me no harm.

I said, "It's okay.
You were just upset.
You said something you didn't mean
And wish you could forget."

I wanted him to know
The depth of my love
And to know that I forgave him
Like our Lord Jesus does.

I want him to always,
As long as he may live,
When he's sorry, go to Jesus
And know that He'll forgive.

His sorrow will be lifted.
He'll no longer have to bear
The guilt for his wrongdoing
After talking to Jesus in prayer.

Jesus accepts his being sorry
And forgives him of his sin
And remembers it no more.
That's when His peace flows in.

How I wish I'd learned this.
My anguish would have ceased.
My life would have been different
Because I'd have known His peace.

We do not need to carry
Our burdens of guilt and sin,
For Jesus will forgive us
If we just invite Him in.

This is being "born again".
It begins our life anew.
Jesus went to the cross to save us,
Something we could never do.

With his love and forgiveness,
He frees us from our strife,
And we'll live forever in Heaven
Where He gives us Eternal Life.

We Should Count Our Blessings

The house is quiet.
The power is out.
Everything I try
Is making me pout.

I can't run any water.
The pump won't work.
All things using water
I'll just have to shirk.

I can't brush my teeth
Or shampoo my hair.
I can't take a shower.
The water's not there.

I'm missing the water
As I walk to the sink.
I'm getting quite thirsty
With no water to drink.

I can't cook anything
On our electric stove.
I can't use our microwave.
This makes me want to rove!

I can't watch TV
Or use a portable phone.
I can't use the computer
To type up this poem.

We can't flush the toilet.
The pump won't run.
At a time like this,
An "outhouse" would be fun!

Our garage door won't open
Automatically,
So I'll just have to lift it
Without electricity.

As I enter a room,
I can't turn on the light.
When the power is out,
Nothing is right!

But today is Sunday,
So off to church I'll go
Without my hair shampooed.
I hope no one will know.

But God will not mind.
He sees me every day,
And it's comforting to know
That He loves me anyway.

Now I'm back from church
And typing up my poem.
The electricity's back on.
Now it feels like home.

We should count the blessings
We take for granted each day,
And appreciate all we have
Before it's taken away.

We must also appreciate
Our husband or wife,
Our children, our loved ones,
And especially our life.

We never know when
Our "light" will go out,
But with Jesus living in us,
His "Light" never goes out.

For, if we believe,
And have Him in our heart,
We'll live on forever.
Believers never part.

Our Church and its Workers

First of all,
We're grateful to God
For Pastor and family
Who are doing a good job.

Our Awana Leaders
And Sunday School Teachers
Encourage our children.
Some may become Preachers.

Fellowship Directors make
Easter Breakfast and Seder.
They help us celebrate
As we gather together.

Committee Secretaries
Take all of the notes,
And Treasurer's record
Where our money goes.

Helpers on Work Day
Have ladders to climb,
To clean, to paint,
And make it a good time.

Our Prayer Chain Leader
Directs the emails
So our prayers are lifted
Up to God without fail.

Christmas baskets for widows,
Who are alone and sad,
Lift their spirits.
For that, we are glad.

Our Pianist and Director,
Whose talent they share,
Make us happy because
We know that they care.

Our Worship Team
Leads all of us in song,
Playing their instruments,
While we sing along.

We're grateful to all
The aforementioned ones
Who all work together
To make our church run.

But we're most grateful
To God up above
For our Savior, Jesus,
And all whom He loves

HOLIDAYS

The inspiration for this poem came to mind on December 15, 1989, as I sat in my car during rush hour waiting for the light to change in the center of our town at the time, Billerica, Massachusetts. I looked out my window and, for the first time that night, noticed the beautiful Christmas lights which decorate the trees on the Common. Because it was such a pleasant surprise, one which I would have missed if I had not been stuck in traffic, this poem started to come to mind.

I went home and wrote the poem. My husband suggested that I share it with others, so I very shyly submitted it to the local newspaper, stating that my husband suggested that I do so. Much to my surprise, that became the first one of my poems to be printed in a newspaper.

<u>Celebrating His Birth</u>

I wonder what our Savior would say
If today He came to earth.
I wonder how He'd like the way
We "celebrate His birth".

He taught of peace and joy and love,
And wants us to be calm.
Instead we shop and push and shove,
And cause each other harm.

Our children long for Christmastime,
Can hardly wait, it seems.
We take our tensions out on them
And shatter all their dreams.

We sit in traffic jams so long,
Our tempers start to flare.
We never even hear the songs
And carols in the air.

We seldom see the colored lights,
So pretty and serene.
We seldom focus on the sights
And think of what they mean.

Let's quietly pause amidst the rush
And really hear the songs.
Let's think of what Christ did for us.
In Christmas, <u>He</u> belongs!

Let's remember that He is alive
And always sees and hears
The way we live at Christmastime
And each day of the year.

I didn't make a notation of what inspired this poem which I wrote on November 26, 1990, but I used it and also my 1989 poem, "Celebrating His Birth," to make our first homemade Christmas cards in 1990.

Teach Them the Meaning

Take time to teach
The little girls and boys:
Christmas is more than
Santa bringing toys.

Christmas is more than
Pretty colored lights
Strung on each house
To brighten our nights.

Christmas is more than
Crowded shopping malls,
And certainly more than
Toy soldiers and dolls.

Christmas is more than
A tall Christmas tree
With presents beneath it
For you and for me.

Christmas is more than
A holiday mood,
And stuffing our tummies
With lots of good food.

Christmas, instead,
Brought us a King,
A Savior to love us
More than anything!

To die for our salvation
Is why He came to earth.
Teach children the reason
We celebrate His birth.

Our church at the time, The First Congregational Church, of Billerica, Massachusetts, had a women's group called The Circle of Friendship. It was my turn to give the devotions at the monthly meeting on December 8, 1990. At the last minute, I decided to write a poem which was whirling around in my mind, based on the first line of a poem by Ernie's grandfather, Arthur Tabor. That first line was: "Pretend you are there on that hillside." I scribbled the poem out very quickly before the meeting and read it there for the devotions. I used the poem for our Christmas cards in 1991.

Following the Savior

Pretend you are there on that hillside.
Pretend you have just seen that star!
Although it's here that you should abide,
Its light beckons you from afar.

There is fear and awe all around you
That to follow it might cause you harm,
But an angel from God reassures you
And restores your peace and calm.

You know you must leave your hillside,
A place that's serene and secure,
To go and follow His Light,
Although you are still unsure.

Your journey is long and frightening,
But you know you are not alone.
The star is brighter than lightning
And urges you to go on.

Then, when the last bend is rounded,
When you get to the Babe in the hay,
You find that your fears were unfounded.
It's there that you want to stay.

That's how it was in those times.
That's how it is today.
When His Light shines into your life,
You'll want to go His way!

Knowing not what awaits you,
Nor what you leave behind,
But knowing that He'll go with you,
Will give you complete peace of mind.

This poem came to me on December 7, 1991, over a year after the events that inspired it.

My husband and children had planned a surprise birthday party for me. A couple of days before my birthday, their actions made me aware that something was going on! The preparations, the cleaning, the whispering, etc., all helped convince me that a party was "in the works"! I started cooperating by helping clean and doing what I could without letting them know of my suspicions. I felt that, the more I helped, the sooner they could relax and spend time with me, which is what I really wanted. The time kept moving on, and they were so preoccupied with their plans that I was feeling left out and a bit resentful. By the time the morning of my birthday arrived and I was still feeling very left out, I was really bitter. I angrily wrote my thoughts on paper as I usually do when I'm upset, which helps me get over those feelings. I ended up having a wonderful birthday party, of course.

Nearly a year later, when I re-read my angry feelings that I had written down that morning, the following poem flowed out of those feelings.

The Birthday Party

They're planning a birthday party for me!
They're frantically working, busy as can be.
They're cooking and cleaning and rushing about.
Why is it that I feel so left out?

They're going out shopping to buy me a gift.
They're hoping to give my spirit a lift.
I know that they love me; of that, there's no doubt.
Why is it that I feel so left out?

They're under such pressure they can't even see
How much I'd rather they spend time with me.
I'm feeling ignored and starting to pout.
I'm tired of feeling completely left out!

The Guest of Honor I'm going to be!
(That is, if they don't forget about me.)
I'll just have to pray and not worry about
The day of my party and being left out.

I'm starting to know, down deep in my heart,
How Jesus feels when we give Him no part
In His birthday party, by rushing about.
Christmas is <u>His</u> birthday! Let's not leave <u>Him</u> out!

"Santa, I've Been Bad"

One day I heard a child saying,
So sad and woefully,
"I have to tell Santa, 'I've been bad',
Which means no gifts for me."

In my heart that caused such aching
To see this child full of dread
And to know this child's heart was breaking
Because of what someone had said.

Now, the original Santa was real.
His name was St. Nicholas, you see.
He was a wonderful Christian
Who lived in 300 A. D.

He didn't want to be worshipped.
His goal was to lead folks to Christ.
He didn't want children to fear him
Nor to know who'd been "naughty or nice".

The Christ that St. Nicholas worshipped
Is there for each person today.
He took all our sins upon Himself
And will wash them all away.

For the forgiveness of all our sins,
He died upon the cross.
None other could love us more
Or, for us, would pay such cost.

There's no need to add up our sins
All year long for a "Santa Claus,"
And to fear that he'll bring us no gifts.
That's nonsense if ever there was!

We must climb up on Jesus' lap
And tell Him we're sorry we sin,
Believe in Him as our Savior,
Open our hearts, and ask Him in.

Some of the gifts He will give us
Are forgiveness, joy, and love;
And peace that, because our Savior arose,
We'll live on in Heaven above.

This poem was inspired by a sermon by Dr. D. James Kennedy's televised sermon in which he made a statement about children correcting us if we were to say, "Rudolph has a green nose."

Christmas Myths

If we jokingly said to most children,
"Rudolph is a green-nosed reindeer,"
They, then, would promptly correct us,
While into our eyes they would peer.

"They'd say, "Why don't you know the difference?
Rudolph has a bright red nose!
How come you've got it all mixed up?
It's something that everyone knows!"

If we jokingly said to these children,
"Santa Claus' suit is blue,"
They'd say, "Don't you know Santa's suit is red?
What is the matter with you?"

If we jokingly said to these children,
"Frosty's a fat old scarecrow,"
They'd wonder what's wrong, and they'd say to us,
"Frosty's a snowman, you know!"

If we seriously said to these children,
"Christmas is more than just toys,"
Would they stare at us in disbelief,
These precious girls and boys?

If we seriously said to these children,
"Christmas is Jesus' birth,"
Would they know anything about Him at all
Or why He came to earth?

Would they know that God sent us a Savior
In the form of that tiny Babe,
That He suffered and died on a cross in our place,
Our eternal lives to save?

They know all the myths about Christmas.
They correct every wrong thing we say.
To make them as sure of the real Truth,
We must teach them about Him today!

The idea for this poem came to me when my husband was reading from a book about how excited the pioneer children were as they waited expectantly for Santa Claus to come. It seemed to me that the real meaning of Christmas, Christ's coming into the world and what He has done for us, should be far more exciting than waiting for Santa Claus' arrival. I didn't know exactly what form this poem should take, but I did some research on the facts about St. Nicholas' life and wrote down some notes about him. These thoughts were in the back of my mind for nearly a year, but how to write the poem didn't come until almost Christmas time the following year, in November of 1992. The figurine of Santa Claus, with hat in hand, kneeling humbly before the Christ Child in the manger, helped to further inspire me as to how I wanted to write this poem. Again, after praying about it, when the time was right, the poem came quickly.

What Would St. Nicholas Say?

What would St. Nicholas say
If he came back to earth today?
I know that his heart would ache.
I think it would probably break.

St. Nicholas, a fine man, you see,
Lived in 300 A. D.
He worked hard and unselfishly,
Converting people to Christianity.

He went all around doing good,
Filling needs wherever he could;
But the world that was full of hate
Imprisoned him for his steadfast faith.

Through the years, they changed his name.
Now "Santa Claus" has all the fame.
People all over the earth
Wait for Santa instead of Christ's birth.

I think that St. Nicholas would say,
If he could come back here today,
"Be joyful, filled with expectancy!
Worship Jesus! Do not worship me!

"Close your chimneys I could not fit in.
Open your hearts invite Jesus in.
The myth of my visits will be gone,
But Jesus' love will live on.

"As it was in the days that I lived,
My whole praise to Jesus I give.
Please celebrate His birth today.
I never meant to get in His way."

All Wrapped Up in Christmas

Christmas is such a busy time
For everyone each year.
The work load seems to get so great
As Christmas time draws near.

Shopping for all the many gifts
To be given to everyone
Creates such a vast amount of work
And keeps us on the run.

Writing to all of our many friends
In the form of a Christmas card
Is a joyful but time consuming task
Which helps make the season hard.

Picking out just the right Christmas tree,
Decorating with many a light,
Cooking and cleaning and rushing about
Suddenly nothing seems right.

Staying up late on Christmas Eve
Tying up all the loose ends,
Tired and nervous, perplexed by it all
It seems like it never ends.

The wrapping of all the gifts that we bought
Goes on and on and on.
We're the ones getting all "wrapped up".
Our Christmas spirit is gone.

It's then that we must take time to pause
And quietly, while we are waiting,
Think about our Lord Jesus Christ,
Whose birth we are celebrating.

Our Savior, Jesus, came to earth
To save us from our sin.
The best gift that we can give ourselves
Is to believe and invite Him in.

Christmas can be as sacred for us
As it was in that manger of hay
When it's "wrapped" around the Christ Child
Like the cloth that wrapped Him that day.

Christmastime Feelings

This Christmas I'm feeling so blessed
With two babies that we're waiting for!
Marcia's baby is due this month--
Christine's in six months more.

This Christmas I'm thinking of Jesus
And the way that He came to earth,
Because our oldest daughter
Is close to giving birth.

This Christmas I'm feeling so close
To Mary, meek and mild,
When she, like our oldest daughter,
Was also "great with child".

This Christmas I'm feeling so sorry
For Mary, who traveled in pain,
Upon an uncomfortable donkey
Through valley, hill and plain.

This Christmas I'm feeling so glad
That in hospitals our daughters can stay,
Unlike the mother of Jesus,
Who gave birth in a stable in hay.

This Christmas I'm feeling relieved
That my daughters will have doctors there,
Unlike that birth in the stable
When it seemed as if nobody cared.

This Christmas I'm feeling so grateful
That these babies will each have a bed;
Whereas, Jesus had only a manger
In which to lay His head.

This Christmas I'm glad for the outfits
Which will cover their tiny forms,
While nothing but swaddling cloths
Kept Baby Jesus warm.

This Christmas I'm feeling so thankful
That, in spite of what we did to Him,
He loves us enough to come into our hearts
And forgive us of our sins.

Do They Know What They're Celebrating?

Do they know what they're celebrating
With all of their decorating?
Thousands and thousands of lights
Adorn their houses at night.

Santa Clauses are glowing.
Everywhere lights are showing.
A bright reindeer pulls a sleigh
Up on the roof and away.

Toy soldiers and candy canes
Glow in the streets and lanes.
Nutcrackers in red and green
Create a colorful scene.

Snowmen so round and fat
Are topped with a big lighted hat.
There's a gingerbread man and his house
And also a Christmas mouse.

I wonder if these people know
What they're celebrating? If so,
Where are the manger scenes--
The truth of what Christmas means?

All that we need today
Is that Child in the manger of hay--
Not just trying to compete
To have the most lights on our street.

Everything covered with lights
Brighten up many nights.
While the lights are lovely to see,
Do they say, "Look at Christ or at me"?

In some homes Christ has no part
In His birthday or in their hearts.
Let's make Christmas what it should be--
Not a showplace for people to see.

Jesus is the "Light of the world"
For each man, woman, boy and girl.
He's the One and the only Light
We need to brighten our day and night.

Please Don't Let Them Rob Us

When we were children,
We could hardly wait
For Christmas to come
On that special date.

We'd see the preparations
The grown-ups would do
To make Christmas special
For me and for you.

We'd help with decorating
The house and Christmas tree
And help with all the cooking
That was done for you and me.

We could hardly wait for a "Santa"
And the gifts that "he" would bring.
How we loved the Christmas lights
And the carols that we'd sing.

Then, as we grew older,
We came to realize
That this was Jesus' birth!
We must see it through His eyes!

Now the world is trying to rob us
Of celebrating His birth,
Of all of Christmas' meaning,
And why He came to earth.

Please don't let them rob our joy:
The carols all around,
The Nativity scene displayed
In the center of each town.

Yes, His birth was special!
Let's stand up to the world;
For Jesus came to save us--
Each man, woman, boy and girl.

The Most Important Gift

When our marriage is blessed
As husband and wife,
God sends our dear children
Into our life.

There's no greater joy
That we've ever known,
Than having these children
Until they are grown.

There's no other love
That is quite as strong
As the way that we love them
All the day long.

Yes, it is difficult
When they want to stray
Away from our teachings
Day after day.

But we always love them
With unconditional love,
The way our Father loves us
From Heaven above.

Because of our love,
We buy lots of gifts--
Toys and trinkets
Their spirits to lift.

Before they are grown,
Our homes overflow--
With abundance of gifts
Everywhere we go.

But we must teach them about Jesus
And how His life He gave.
Because He loved them so,
He died so they'd be saved.

When they are older,
We love them no less.
We love them as adults
With the deepest closeness.

We still want to give them
Gifts from our love,
As our Father in Heaven
Sends His gifts from above.

What's the most important
Gift we can give,
That will give our children peace
As long as they live?

To know that we love Jesus,
And He's also in their hearts;
So, when our lives are ended,
We will never part.

When they stand at our grave
And know we're not there,
But we're living in Heaven,
Takes away their despair.

When they live out their lives
Knowing we believed,
It will give them perfect peace--
The best gift we can leave.

What Christmas Means to Me

When I was a child
And Christmas was near,
I'd be eagerly waiting
For the gifts I'd get that year.

Then, as I grew older,
The new joy of living
Was not in the receiving,
But in the gift giving.

Many years later,
I came to realize
The true meaning of Christmas
And how it changes lives.

That first Christmas we received
The greatest Gift ever given--
In God's love, He came as Jesus
To lead us all to Heaven.

God knew we were not able
To save ourselves alone.
Jesus went to the cross for us.
There our sins He atoned.

For me, this new awakening
Brought joy that will not cease,
When Jesus changed my life
And gave me inner peace.

Now my only wish for Christmas,
And each day of the year,
Is that everyone will receive
That Gift I hold so dear.

And so, this Christmas season,
I pray that in Jesus you'll believe,
And ask Him for forgiveness,
So His peace you will receive.

Then, because He arose on Easter,
If you have Him in your heart,
You, too, will live in Heaven where
Believing loved ones never part.

Never A Mention

As Christmas approaches,
We're filled with glee,
Buying and decorating
Our Christmas tree.

We're shopping and wrapping
All of our gifts.
This Christmas season
Gives our spirits a lift.

We're writing and sending
Our Christmas cards
To loved ones and friends
Both near and far.

We're busily cooking
Our holiday food,
Tasting now and then,
Making sure that it's good.

Then Christmas arrives
With presents galore
Under the tree and
Around on the floor.

Everyone races through
The opening of gifts
With never a mention
Of God's greatest Gift.

Never a mention
Of Jesus' name,
Never a mention
Of why He came,

Never a mention
That the Son of God
Came to be our Savior,
Came to be our Lord.

Never a mention
Of Whose birth it was,
We're only focusing
On Santa Claus......

How must Jesus feel
When His life He gave
For each one of us
Whom He came to save?

If we ask His forgiveness
And turn from our sins,
He'll give us his peace
When we invite him in.

Christmas Cards

I love the Christmas season,
Especially the Christmas cards.
I love hearing from our friends
And loved ones, both near and far.

Each day I can hardly wait
To go to the mailbox to see
Who will be sending greetings
To us and our family.

Some cards come from people
We see almost every day.
Many others come from folks
Who live very far away.

I especially love the news
Of each sender's family
That they send in their newsletters.
They mean so much to me.

The pictures and poems they send
Are displayed for our family
To share the joy with each other.
That's what Christmas should be.

Then, when Christmas has passed,
I always feel let down.
When going to the mailbox,
Regular mail and bills make me frown!

So, this season, as always,
I'll send a poem to you
And remind you of Jesus' birth
And how much He loves you.

And I'll ask you once again,
As I tend to do every year,
To send us all your news.
It's what we love to hear.

How We Celebrate Christmas

Each year we come together,
Our entire family,
And we all gather around
Our special Christmas tree.

We sing "Happy Birthday" to Jesus.
The children can hardly wait
To blow out all of the candles
And eat His birthday cake.

Before we open our presents,
We remember Jesus' birth
By reading from the Bible about
The night He came to earth.

Then I pick up Jesus in His manger
From beneath the Christmas tree
And tell the children the story
Of His love for them and for me.

I tell them that we must love Him,
Believe in Him and be reborn,
Then tell everyone about Him;
So I ask them to pass Him on.

We then pass the manger around
From one person to another--
Accepting Jesus and passing Him to
Each father, mother, sister, and brother.

Doing this represents
What God has told us to do:
To tell everyone about Jesus
And how much He loves you.

He loved each of us so much
That His earthly life He gave.
Then He arose and lives on--
Our eternal lives to save.

Just Imagine!

In the book of Luke in our Bible,
In Chapter 2, verses 9 through 11,
Fearful shepherds heard this announcement
From an angel descending from Heaven.

"Fear not: for, behold,
I bring you good tidings
of great joy, which shall
be to all people. For unto
you is born this day in the
city of David a Saviour
which is Christ the Lord."

Just imagine! Just imagine
An angel coming to earth!
Just imagine being told by an angel
Of this Holy Baby's birth!

Just imagine being told
That this tiny Baby Boy
Would be Jesus Christ, our Saviour!
Just imagine! Imagine the joy!

Just imagine God in His Trinity
Loving us so very much.
Knowing we could not save ourselves,
He came as one of us!

He came to take all of our sins
Upon Himself to the cross;
So, believing in Him, we'll live on.
To death we will not be lost!

Can you possibly imagine
Someone loving us enough
To die in our place so we can live?
Jesus loves us this much!

So let's imagine being with the shepherds
The night that angel came to earth.
Let's be filled with awe like they were
As we celebrate Jesus' birth!

Merry Christmas!

"Merry Christmas!" "Merry Christmas!"
Let's say it every day.
"Merry Christmas!" Let's keep saying it
To each person along the way.

The world is trying to rob us
Of the privilege to say,
"Merry Christmas." It's no longer allowed.
We're to say, "Happy Holidays."

But Christians are not celebrating
Just "holidays" here on earth.
Christians are celebrating
Our dear Lord Jesus Christ's birth!

No, it isn't just a holiday.
For us, He changed our life!
God came as a Baby through Mary,
Joseph's betrothed wife.

If it were not for Jesus,
Our Lord, our Savior, our King,
We'd be born, and we'd die in our sins.
Our lives wouldn't mean anything.

But, because Jesus went to the cross
To die for our sins in our place,
If we'll just believe in Him,
All of our sins He'll erase.

Not only will they be erased,
When through Christ our sins are forgiven,
We will receive His peace that
When we die, we'll live on in Heaven!

So, World, don't try to tell us,
As we travel along our way,
To dishonor Christ Jesus' birth
By just saying, "Happy Holidays!"

We'll keep on saying, "Merry Christmas."
The word "Christmas" begins with Christ!
We'll honor our Lord and Savior
Who gives us eternal life!

Christmas Season and It's Reason

Oh, Dear Lord,
What a tough year it's been--
Losing loved ones
Again and again.

But how comforting to know
That believers who are gone
Are there with You
In Heaven living on.

Even our churches
Suffer many a loss
That cause us to come
To the foot of the cross.

We lay at Your Feet
Our burdens and then
Ask You to help us
Once again.

That is the reason
Why You came to earth--
To save us all
Through your Holy Birth.

You died on the cross
There in our place
For our forgiveness,
Our sins to erase.

When we come to believe,
Such peace we are given
Knowing that when we die,
We will live on in Heaven.

If we believe in Jesus
And ask Him into our heart,
We'll join our believing loved ones.
In Heaven we'll never part.

So, Father, I ask You
During every Christmas season,
Help us to concentrate on
Jesus Christ, the Reason.

Our Christmas Celebration

Each one of us rises early
With so much that we must do
To prepare a special meal
For all loved ones coming through.

Our hearts fill with anticipation
While we wait for them to arrive,
Preparing our Christmas meal
And happy to be alive.

We've shopped for all of our loved ones
For each one's special gifts.
Waiting to see each gift opened
Always gives our spirits a lift.

We must be sure to remember
The meaning of this special day.
It's not just the meal or the gifts
Of which memories soon fade away.

The day should be filled with gratitude
For the greatest gift ever given:
When our Lord and Savior was born
And belief in Him takes us to Heaven.

Easter's Real Meaning

My heart starts to ache
When I realize,
Some children know Easter
Only through worldly eyes.

Easter bunnies and chickens
Are not "where it's at,"
Nor a pretty new dress
Or a flowery hat.

Baskets full of candy
That the "Easter Bunny" brought
Won't teach Easter's meaning
To one tiny tot.

Coloring Easter eggs
Sure can be fun,
But what have we taught them
When the eggs are all done?

Please, I beseech you,
Before all is lost,
Teach them about Jesus
Who died on the cross.

It was on Good Friday
He hung on that tree
For the forgiveness of sinners
Like you and like me.

On Easter, Hallelujah,
Our Savior arose!
On all who believe,
Eternal Life He bestows.

So please, everyone,
For all those you love,
Teach them about
Our Savior above.

The Tomb Became a Womb

It was on Good Friday
Jesus was crucified.
With our sins upon Him,
He suffered and died.

Like all who are dead,
He was placed in a tomb;
But instead of a grave,
It became a womb!

Through the rest of Good Friday
And all of Saturday,
Jesus' dead body
In the tomb did lay.

On Sunday morning
From the tomb He was gone.
He'd been resurrected,
From this "womb" reborn!

He'd been buried with our sins
From all of our strife.
Instead of a tomb of death,
It had become a womb of life.

The same thing will happen
To each of us when
We die to our sins.
We'll be born again.

Jesus' death and resurrection
Was for me and for you.
From our sins we must die
To be born anew.

When we ask His forgiveness,
Our sins will be gone;
And because He arose,
We, too, will live on.

On June 11, 1995, our pastor, Rev. Nelson Elliott, at the First Baptist Church of Shapleigh, Maine, said in his sermon how sad he feels when he is marching in a parade as a Fire Chaplain and no one salutes the American flag when it passes by. I wrote this poem on June 19, 1995. It has been enclosed with the church bulletin several times since it was written. Now a member of our church, Ed Stubbs, is setting it to music and will sing it this year before the Fourth of July.

The Fourth of July

As we are approaching
The Fourth of July,
We're anticipating
Parades going by.

American flags will be
Flying and proud,
Carried along past the
Huge gathered crowd.

If these flags could talk,
I think they would say,
"Where's the respect
Like in earlier days?

"We used to be honored
Through peace and through strife,
Millions being willing
To give up their life.

"Young children today
Are not being taught
How lives were lost
For the freedom we've got.

"Now people can't even
Be bothered to salute.
As we're passing by,
They don't give a hoot.

"So, stand up, America!
Take off that hat!
Place your hand on your heart!
It's as easy as that!

"It's not much to ask
Just one little prod:
Let's get back to being
One nation under God."

God Bless America

With rumors of war overshadowing us
And terrorist plots here and there,
Our patriotism has been re-ignited:
"God Bless America" signs everywhere.

I wonder how God is feeling right now.
I wonder what He'd have to say.
With the kind of lives that we are living,
We still want to have it our way.

He might say to each of us here on Earth:
"You don't want Me in your school.
You won't allow any mention of Me
Or even the Golden Rule.
      But you want Me to bless America?

"You don't want Me in your government
Which was established by Me.
You think church and state should be
    separate.
That's not what was meant to be!
      But you want Me to bless America?

"You never want to go to church.
You want to keep living in sin.
You want to keep doing what you want to do
And never invite Me in.
      But you want Me to bless America?

"You won't accept the miraculous gifts
That I have been sending to you--
Millions of babies killed in the womb--
That breaks My heart in two!
      But you want Me to bless America?

"You don't want to have Me in your homes.
You just want to live your own way--
Unmarried and living together's not right,
Nor living together and gay.
      But you want Me to bless America?

"The kind of entertainment you choose
Is so offensive to Me.
The murders, the sex and the violence
Are not what I want you to see.
      But you want Me to bless America?

"I think, before you put up your signs,
Perhaps you should look within
And examine your life as seen through My
    eyes;
And turn away from your sin.

"I truly want to bless all of you
And forgive you of your sins.
I love you; I'm knocking; and I'm waiting.
Please invite Me back in.
      <u>Then</u> ask Me to bless America!"

This poem was written on November 18, 1991, after a woman in our Bible Study indicated that she was dreading Thanksgiving because she didn't have anything to be thankful for.

Be Thankful

As we approach Thanksgiving Day,
Let us all take time to pray,
And count our blessings, rich or poor,
That we can all be thankful for:

Be thankful for each day's sunrise,
And love that shines through children's eyes.
Be thankful for each set of sun,
So lovely when the day is done.

Be thankful for the stars that gleam,
And ocean, mountain, lake, and stream.
Be thankful for the air so free,
And for each flower, plant, and tree.

Be thankful for the sky above,
And grateful for the ones we love.
Be thankful for the universe,
And for our God Who loved us first.

Be thankful that in our Lord's grace,
He went to Calvary in our place
To forgive our sins so we may be
Living on eternally.

The list goes on if we just try
To keep an open mind and eye.
We find that blessings do abound
If we just stop and look around!

HUMOR

I'm not sure when this happened because I just wrote the month, day and time, but not the year. What I had written on it was March 16, 2:00 a.m. I think it was probably 1987, a few months after I had been baptized in 1986.

This was the first poem that ever came to me when I was sleeping soundly. I awoke and the poem was still whirling around in my mind. I was exhausted, but intrigued and amused, so I dragged myself out of bed, went downstairs still half asleep and bleary-eyed, fumbled around for a paper and pencil, and wrote it down because I knew I would never remember it in the morning. I also knew that I wouldn't remember it because it is not something that I had ever thought about nor would have written about. It just seemed to be a dumb little poem, but people who hear it now think it's cute. I had no way of knowing that this was the beginning of many more such instances when my sleep would be interrupted by this "nudging" to get up and write. It isn't always easy because I like my sleep, and getting out of a warm, cozy bed to go down to a cool living room in the wee hours of the morning isn't always appealing! But I know that I have to do it because, when I don't, the poem is completely gone from my mind in the morning.

I have since learned that this may have been a test from the Lord to see whether or not I would be faithful to this first "nudging" that He gave me. Since I was faithful in this instance, He has sent many, many more poems through me.

This reminds me of the passage in Matthew, 25:23 which speaks of the talents given to a person by his master: "His master replies, "Well done, good and faithful servant! You have been faithful with a few things; I will put you in charge of many things. Come and share your master's happiness!" And, for me, there is indeed great happiness when I realize that He has sent another poem or writing through me.

Sidewalk Smile

The friendly look of a sidewalk smile
Makes you stop and ponder a while.

A little boy came walking by
And found cement that was not dry.

An urge too great for him to resist
Formed his hand into a fist.

With index finger pointed out
He drew a face that will never pout.

This "smiley face," no accident,
Preserved forever in dry cement!

On August 2, 1988, my father, Donald Folsom, called me and told me a cute story that had amazed him while he was mowing his lawn. During that night, at 4:30 a.m., the following poem came to me and I got up and wrote it.

Donald and the Frog

There sat dear old kindly Don,
Riding along, mowing his lawn.

But the story isn't over yet:
He felt his leg becoming wet!

This puzzled him because he knew
That it was something he didn't do!

He got off the mower, still in a fog,
Pulled out his pockets and out jumped a frog!

He went in the house like a little boy
And told his wife the wildest story

About the frog that got away
And left him with wet pants that day!

In 1994 I was serving one of my two terms as a Deaconess at the First Baptist Church of Shapleigh in Maine. On June 6 of that year, I was attending our regular Deacon's meeting on the Monday night following the previous day's serving of Communion. One of the other Deacons, Loren Kannenburg, complimented me on one of my poems that he had recently read. He was a quiet man and, with a twinkle in his eye, he said, "Why don't you write a poem about bugs?" I said that I wasn't sure I would be able to write one. He mentioned all of the black flies that were currently infiltrating Maine as they do each year. I really didn't think I would write one, but when I got home, the following poem began forming in my mind. I ended up having a poem to give Loren after all. He was pleased and amused by it.

A Poem About Bugs!

Loren suggested that
I try to write
A poem about bugs,
So I'll try it tonight.

He thought that, because
It's summer in Maine,
I should write about bugs
Because they're such a pain!

To write about bugs,
Where do I begin?
Maybe with mosquitoes
Who light upon our skin.

Mosquitoes come humming
Their annoying tune.
We whack them and chase them
Around the whole room!

But they always win
The battle in which
They give us a bite
Which causes an itch!

Now how about flies
Who buzz in our ears?
When we get the swatter,
They always disappear!

Then there are black flies
Who fly in a swarm
All around our heads
On nights that are warm.

Then, of course, there are
Thousands of ants,
Indoors and outdoors,
But not in our pants!

When I started this poem,
I didn't think I could write
This many verses
About bugs tonight!

But God always helps me,
Even writing about bugs!
But I think I'd rather be
Writing about hugs!

Don's In Trouble Again!

Don got himself into trouble again
As he quite often does!
But this is one of the weirdest yet,
The funniest that ever was!

He got out of bed one morning
Couldn't find his bottom teeth!
He often pops them out at night,
But finds them within his reach.

But this day, when he got up,
He searched all over the bed.
He couldn't find his teeth!
His face was turning red!

He called his good wife, Beulah,
Who always helps him out.
They looked all around the room.
Now he was beginning to pout!

They searched throughout the morning
And continued 'till after noon.
They couldn't figure it out
"Those teeth must be in this room."

So Don tried one more time
Looked around the room once more.
He suddenly noticed something that
He hadn't seen before.

On the floor in front of the closet
Were a couple pairs of shoes.
"Those teeth couldn't be over there,
But what have I got to lose?"

He walked over to the shoes
And moved them around a bit.
There, under one of the shoes were
The teeth hidden under it!

He'd popped them out onto the blanket
Which was thrown off with a lurch.
They'd flown down under the shoe
And had given him quite a search!

There must be a moral written
Into this little rhyme:
"God helps those who help themselves,"
But in His very own time!

This was written about my eighty-four-year-old mother, Beulah Folsom, in November of 1995 to be read at my parents' 60th anniversary celebration on November 27 at the Blue Door Inn in Alfred, Maine. This is about an encounter with a bear that she had earlier that year in the woods behind their house in Butlers' Corner in Springvale, Maine.

Beulah and the Bear

One night Don and Beulah were watching T.V.
A special show about bears.
They made the comment that neither of them
Had ever seen a bear.

The next morning Beulah went out for a walk
To breathe in some fresh air.
But what did she get instead that day?
A visit with a bear!

She had walked up to the top of the hill.
She wanted to calmly stare
At the trees that the men had been cutting
Not a visit with a bear!

While she was standing there looking,
She seemed to feel the hair
Starting to stand on the back of her neck
She turned and saw the bear!

The bear had just come from the river.
He'd gotten a drink down there.
Beulah was not pleased to see him
And neither was the bear!

They both stood and looked at each other.
To move, Beulah didn't dare.
The bear finally took off running
I guess she gave him a scare!

The feeling was certainly mutual,
Neither was happy there;
Beulah with her heart pounding
Nor her visiting black bear!

We're grateful that God was present
Between the two of them there;
And now, all that's left is a memory of
Beulah's visit with a bear.

Beulah and the Bat

One night Beulah was sleeping
Peacefully in her bed,
When suddenly she heard a bat
Circling around her head!

She got out of bed and chased him
Around and around the room!
She thought that she would have to
Go downstairs to get the broom.

Then the bat flew into the hall.
Beulah slammed the door.
She went back to bed, got back to sleep,
And worried about him no more.

The next night, at bedtime, she dreaded
To begin another plight
Of possibly chasing the bat again
And ruining another night.

But Don told her not to worry--
"The bat's probably not in your room."
So she went up the stairs to spend the night
Sleeping in her bedroom.

In the morning she washed the dishes,
Then walked away from the dish pan.
Don was going to empty it for her
And reached into it with his hand.

Immediately something grabbed him
Which really startled Don!
(You don't think anything in your dish pan
Will grab your hand and hold on!)

It was the bat in really bad shape.
In fact, he was nearly drowned.
They took him out into their back yard,
And he started to jump up and down.

He finally flew up on their well
And to the side he hung on.
A little while later, when they looked,
The bat was finally gone.

Don and Beulah relaxed completely
At the end of their ordeal.
They went back into their house
And finished eating their meal.

Hopefully this ends the story
And the bat will not find his way
Back into their house tonight.
For this we all will pray.

Something A Grandmother Will Understand

You may ask me why
I'm so full of joy.
It's because of a call
From a three-year-old boy.

I was riding along
Alone in my car,
When I heard my cell phone
Ringing from afar.

After I reached it
And answered the call,
I then heard the sweetest
Sound of them all.

With a deep, raspy voice
Sounding very loud,
He wanted to tell me
Why he was so proud.

Too innocent to know
That the subject matter,
If discussed in some circles,
Would cause drinks to splatter!

But he warmed my heart
As we talked to each other.
I was glad God allowed me
To be a grandmother.

Why can't I stop smiling
In my car doing forty?
Because he shouted, "Grammie,
I pooped on the potty!"

Those Annoying Flies!

When flies are born,
From birth they are taught
Many, many things--
What to "do" and "do not".

When they are older,
They go to Fly School.
There they learn much,
But not the Golden Rule.

Their most important classes
When school has begun,
Are found in a course called
"Fly Swatter 101".

Very early on,
The first thing they learn
Is about fly swatters
And how to dart and turn.

They study fly swatters
From morning till night
And how to avoid them,
Darting left and right.

They learn swatter's shapes
So they will know.
The minute we grab one,
Into hiding they'll go.

They also are taught
Where they can light
So we cannot whack them
And cause a terrible sight.

We can't strike them on mirrors
Because they will break,
Nor on fragile ornaments
That would cause hearts to ache.

And we cannot strike them
On a plate filled with food.
A dead fly in our meal
Will destroy our mood!

So we must live with them,
These annoying flies.
They're a part of our lives.
How our patience they try!

God must have created
These flies for a reason
To strengthen our patience
During every fly season!

Why, Oh Why?

Why, oh why,
I ask day and night,
Does anyone want
A floor that is white?

Who wants a floor
On which you walk
That shows every particle,
Shows every spot,

Everything you drop,
Every little hair?
Everywhere you look,
You see it all there.

The dirt that comes in
Gets tracked all around
And leaves the white floor
Looking mostly brown.

You clean the spots.
You mop and mop.
You fret and fuss.
You clean till you drop.

Your time is wasted
Cleaning over and over
When you could be outside
Admiring the clover.

You could be making
Better use of your time
Using God-given talent
To write little rhymes!

You could be enjoying
Special time with a child,
Watching him playing
And running wild;

And more important,
Spending time with the Lord,
Working or teaching
That child about God.

So, what I am wondering is,
"Why would it hurt
If the color of the floor
Were the color of dirt?"

LIFE LESSONS

I wrote this poem in four minutes on April 7, 1994, after returning to my home in Billerica, Massachusetts, after my morning walk. That day it was raining quite hard. I was carrying my yellow umbrella and was staying dry under it. Suddenly I noticed that the gray, dreary day had taken on a sunny hue. I looked up and realized that it was because of the light shining through my yellow umbrella. The day was no brighter than it had been earlier, but it seemed brighter after I noticed it and all of the other blessings around me.

My "Yella" Umbrella

When the day is rainy
And gray as it can get,
Take out your umbrella
And you won't get wet.

Why stay at home
And get all depressed?
Go out for a walk
After getting yourself dressed.

Outdoors there under
The gray cloudy sky
Are things that you wouldn't
Notice when dry.

The birds are still singing
As happy as can be
Way up very high
In the tallest oak tree.

The flowers are still blooming.
They love the rain.
They're saying, "Thank you,"
To God once again.

The people driving by
May stare for a while;
But just stare right back,
And give them a smile!

One thing I especially
Noticed today
While I was walking,
"My clouds" went away.

You may not believe this
Or think that it's funny
Under my "yella" umbrella,
The sky appears sunny!

This poem was written on April 27, 1994. It was also written in five minutes after returning from my walk that morning.

Lessons from a Mockingbird

Where is he hiding?
I cannot see
The mocking bird singing
Up high in some tree.

His music so pleasant,
So wondrous to hear,
Is joyfully wending
Its way to my ear.

I slow down my steps
As I walk along
Hoping to see the
Source of that song.

But he keeps on hiding
And toying with me.
It seems like he knows
And it fills him with glee!

So I just stop looking
And walk on along
Enjoying the mockingbird's
God-given song.

This can be taken as
A lesson to me:
God's blessings surround us,
Even those we can't see.

At 3:00 a.m. on June 2, 1995, I was awakened by a loudly singing mockingbird in a tree near our open bedroom window. As much as I love to listen to the many songs of a mockingbird during the day, this one was annoying until I finished writing the poem and changed my attitude to one of seeing the blessing.

That Pesky Mockingbird

How I love the mockingbird.
He surely is a glorious bird.
God gave to him many a song.
I love to hear him all day long.

Whenever he's singing during the day,
I point him out to friends on the way.
I have them listen to his singing there.
His blessing with them I want to share.

Then comes the time he wants to date
All night he serenades his mate.
His song is glorious then, it's true;
But, so is my sleep, I wish he knew!

I wonder if she feels the same way
Saying, "I'd rather you'd sing to me during the day!
I'm tired right now and needing some sleep.
I'll listen tomorrow; but, for now, shut your beak!"

I love his singing every day.
At night, I wish he'd go away!
How I wish that he would keep
His beak closed when I'm trying to sleep!

What moral can I learn from this?
Its lesson I don't want to miss
I'm not quite sure, but I am guessing
Your heart must be open to accept God's blessing.

For I do not really want him to leave.
His lovely songs I will gladly receive.
If I put aside my desire to sleep,
God's blessing I will surely keep.

Now that I have had my say,
He's singing a little farther away.
That is better, I must admit.
I'll go back to bed and enjoy it!

A Neat, Clean House

How do we get
Our house to stay
Neat and clean
Nearly every day?

The following are
A few little rules
To help us to do it.
They're really cool!

"What belongs
On the kitchen floor?
Linoleum, pet dishes,
Shoes and boots by the door.

"What on the kitchen
Counter belongs?
Utensils and appliances,
Washed dishes, not for long.

"What belongs
In the kitchen sink?
The answer to this
Is, 'Nothing,' I think.

"What belongs
On the other rooms' floors?
Carpets and furniture
And nothing more.

"What belongs
On the living room furniture?
Cushions and pillows
And nothing else there.

"What belongs
On the table tops?
Pictures and knickknacks.
No more there should you
    drop.

"What belongs
On any stairs?
Nothing! It's dangerous!
Pick it up if it's there!

"What belongs
On our bedroom floors?
Furniture only,
Clothes in closets and
    drawers.

"What belongs
On our beds every day?
Only pillows and bedspreads
On beds freshly made.

"What belongs
In the kids' rooms each day?
Beds also made,
Toys and clothes put away.

"What belongs
In our bathrooms each day?
Waste cans emptied daily,
All things used put away.

"What belongs
On the laundry room floor?
Hampers, clothes baskets
And nothing more."

I'm also thinking
Of some other rules:
"If you drop it, pick it up."
That's really cool.

"If you use it, you should
Put it back when you're
    done."
Keeping things neat
Can really be fun.

I learned as a child
The most important one:
"Once a job is begun,
Never leave it till it's done."

When using these rules,
You'll see what I mean:
When our house is neat,
It's easy to clean.

A way to get it neat
And to keep it that way:
Use three bins: "Trash,"
    "Keep,"
And "Give Away."

God gave us our homes.
Our homes He does bless.
But I don't think He wants
    them
To be a big mess!

These are things I've learned
Along the way,
But I still struggle
With them every day!

It's Okay

I held a little toddler today.
His mother had gone to a meeting.
He couldn't understand why she'd gone away.
His heart was rapidly beating.

When his mother left, he started to cry.
I hugged him and said, "It's okay."
The tears were flowing down his cheeks.
With a tissue, I wiped them away.

The panic was showing on his little face.
He looked around and then reached up to me.
I picked him up and held him close
Then sat down with him on my knee.

His crying stopped as he clutched his toy dog,
And I hugged him close on my lap.
As the time passed, he became quite tired;
But he couldn't relax and nap.

No one could convince him to leave me that day.
The other little girls and boys
Would come and ask him to get down and play
With them and with all of the toys.

From time to time, he'd look up at me--
His wide eyes filling with tears.
I'd hug him tighter and say, "It's okay."
That was all that he needed to hear.

The only time that he would move
While we sat there two hours and more,
Was when his toy dog would slip from his grasp
And fall down onto the floor.

When I'd put him down to pick up the dog,
His panic would come back and then,
I'd pick him up and hold him close
And say, "It's okay," again.

His mom came back as I told him she would--
A promise he found hard to believe.
For him it felt like forever,
But he waited and trusted me.

This caused me to think about each one of us
And the fears that we face every day.
We need to climb up on Jesus' lap.
He'll hold us and say, "It's okay."

R. S. V. P.

The invitation says "R. S. V. P.,"
"Repondez s'il vous plait,"
The French words that mean, "Please respond" if you wish
To be present on that day.

For the people planning the event,
This is what they need
To know how many people will attend--
How many they'll have to feed.

There are many people who are much too arrogant
To feel that they need to reply.
They feel there's always room for them,
So they let their response slip by.

When they arrive at the event,
There's no place set for them at the table.
When they're told that they must be turned away,
They plead as much as they're able.

But, at the door they were turned away.
No food for them had been cooked.
A place at the table wasn't set because
Their name wasn't in the book.

For us, the same thing applies to Heaven.
When we are alive, our Lord sends
An invitation to all those He loves
For the instant when our life ends.

He invites each of us to come unto Him--
To respond and ask him into our hearts,
To join Him and our believing loved ones
In Heaven where we'll never part.

When we accept His invitation
That is our R. S. V. P.
He writes our name in His Book of Life,
And He welcomes us instantly.

For all of those who are much too arrogant
And think they don't need to respond,
Since there are only two destinations,
To "the other place" they must move on.

Take Refuge

After a forest fire, a man found
A black, charred lump lying on the ground.
He approached it but could not identify
What it was, so he nearly walked by.

On closer examination, he learned
That it was a large bird nearly half burned.
He wondered as he looked at the bird where
it lay
Why from the fire it had not flown away.

As he pushed the bird aside with his foot,
Its body all charred and covered with soot,
What he found when he pushed it aside,
Was something so beautiful, he nearly cried.

Under the body was such a surprise,
He blinked and could hardly believe his
eyes:
Hovering together were several baby birds.
He was so stunned that he couldn't find
words.

When the mother bird had sensed danger
was near,
She had cautioned each baby to, "Come
over here!"
She covered them safely under her wings,
Then settled herself for what the future
would bring.

To save herself, she could have flown,
But she chose instead to save her own.
Each baby who obeyed her call to come
Was saved that day when they chose not to
run.

The man looked beyond, where ten feet
away,
Lay a charred baby bird that died that day.
Such sorrow was borne by the mother bird
For the one chick who chose not to come to
her.

This story reminds us of Christ, our Lord.
He could have escaped because He is God.
But He loved us so much, His life He gave
So that each one who obeys Him will be
saved.

God is our refuge in everything.
He gathers us under His protective wings.
When He invites each of us to come,
Into His loving arms we must run.

Psalm 57 speaks of the shadow of His wings
Which give us refuge in everything.
In Isaiah 43, we can learn:
When we walk through the fire, we will not
be burned.

But each one of us His call must obey.
We cannot be saved if we run away.
Our only two choices are Hell or Heaven:
Burning in Hell or living in Heaven

Happy New Year

When the old year is gone,
What people say
Is "Happy New Year"
On the new year's first day.

When people say it,
They're usually grinning,
Happy and hopeful
As the new year's beginning.

They make resolutions
That they're going to try,
Hoping to change things
From the year that's gone by.

They resolve to lose weight.
They resolve to stop drinking.
They resolve to stop smoking.
They try a new way of thinking.

However, their resolutions
Don't last very long.
Their habits soon come back.
Everything seems wrong.

They feel like they've failed.
It happens every year.
They've gained weight. They're smoking.
They're again drinking beer.

A popular resolution
That many people make
Is to be a better person,
But they soon make old mistakes.

There's only one way
Our lives can change. It's when
We repent of our sins
And we are "born again".

We must believe in Jesus,
Turn away from our sins,
Ask Him for forgiveness,
Open our heart and invite Him in.

Suddenly the changed life
That we're looking for each year,
Will be ours forever
While Jesus holds us near.

The peace we've searched for
Year after year and failed
Will be ours because our sins
To His cross have been nailed.

So, instead of "Happy New Year,"
And resolutions that cease,
Pray this year to be born again
So you'll finally know His peace.

A Woman's Titles

A woman has titles
From before she is born:
Embryo, fetus,
The list goes on.

When she is born
Her title is baby.
Tiny and adorable,
She's a cute little lady.

In a couple of years,
She's a toddler so fine.
Then her title is child
Until she's about nine.

From nine through twelve,
She's now called a tween,
A new title for her till
At thirteen she's a teen.

At twenty she's no longer
Called a teenager.
She's now a young woman
Feeling grown up, I'll wager.

On her twenty-first birthday,
She's called and adult.
A definite grown-up
Is this birthday's result.

At some point in her life,
When she puts her faith in God,
She becomes a Christian
Saved by Jesus, her Lord.

When she gets a job title,
She's a nurse or a teacher,
A doctor, a lawyer,
A secretary or preacher.

When she meets a young man,
Falls in love some day,
And they get engaged,
She becomes a fiancée.

When these two marry,
She becomes a bride,
Hand in hand together
At her new husband's side.

After they marry,
She is now a wife,
A title she hopes to carry
The rest of her life.

When their children come along,
She is now called Mother.
This title brings such joy
As they love one another.

When people look to her
On tough days that never end,
She listens with her heart
Because she is a friend.

Then, as she grows older,
Her heart is filled with joy.
She's now a grandmother
To precious girls and boys.

But just before this happens,
She gets a title that is tough--
One that people joke about--
One which makes life rough.

That deeply dreaded title
Is the one called mother-in-law.
Ridiculed and despised by many,
That title "sticks in her craw."

It's a name that she should love
Because of what it means:
She's now blessed with new children,
But the world now calls her mean.

So please give her a chance
To prove to those she loves
That she wants to be accepted
As a person they can love.

If Only I'd Known

If only I'd known
You'd be going away,
I'd have stopped by to see you
Every day.

If only I'd known
That you couldn't stay,
I'd have treasured our moments
Day after day.

If only I'd known,
As we went through our days,
How swiftly time passes
It's that way always.

If only I'd known
That, for such a long while,
I'd be missing your twinkling
Eyes and warm smile.

If only I'd known
How much time I'd wasted,
Not being with you
Sharing joy we had tasted.

If only I'd known,
In all kinds of weather,
I should value the time
That we had together.

If only I'd known
That you'd soon pass away,
Leaving me missing you
More day by day.

But, praise God, I <u>know</u>
That I'll see you one day
In our eternal
Home far away.

For that, Jesus promised,
Will be our reward,
If we but repent
And believe He is Lord.

Facebook

Facebook's a form of communication
To stay connected with friends.
The list of people who are using it now
Seems as if it will never end.

Whenever they want to write to their friends,
Who are nearly always there,
They can communicate anytime
And communicate anywhere.

They can share their friends with others
Who, in turn, become friends.
The list continues to keep on growing
With each one adding new friends.

This reminds us of Jesus Christ,
Our Lord, our Savior, our Friend:
When we tell others about God's Son,
And they accept Him as their Friend.

One way in which this greatly differs
From the Facebook list of friends:
People can be "unfriended" on Facebook
If they're no longer wanted as friends.

How humiliating to be "unfriended,"
As they see it there in print,
And learn that their friendship has been rejected
Without being given a hint.

One thing that they can always count on:
From His list, God will never "unfriend"!
Unless they continue rejecting His Son,
On His "Friends" list, they'll stay without end.

PARENTING

How Time Flies

I can't believe where the time has gone
Or how quickly the years have flown,
From the time that our three children were
   born
Till the time that they left home.

An apartment was home when our first child
   was born.
When she was six months old, we moved
To a white cape and garage with a great big
   lawn--
A good investment it proved.

She slept in our room for many a day.
Then we moved her to her own room.
I cried when she moved so "far away".
My world was filled with gloom.

Two years later our son was born,
And in our bedroom he stayed.
Then it was time for him to move on
Into that room "far away".

Of course, that aforementioned "far away"
   room
Was not far away at all--
Just a walk through the living room into the
   room
On the other side of our wall!

Four years later, coming our way
Was our child number three.
Our house needed to be expanded quickly
While our hearts were full of glee.

Then, when this youngest girl was born,
Our rooms nearly finished upstairs,
She slept in our room from that time on
Until we could all move up there.

Every time that we took the crib down
And in another room set up their bed,
You'd think that the child was leaving town
By all of the tears that I shed!

It seems that we hardly got settled when
   time
Just flew so quickly by;
And now they're all grown and moved out,
   and I'm
Just having a final cry.

The rooms that we added are now sitting still
And quiet as we pass by.
We'd just gotten them finished, and now
   they're empty.
Oh, how the time does fly.

But God in His goodness does help us to
   make
The best of life's phases and then,
Retirement and grandchildren are not hard
   to take!
The cycle starts over again.

This poem was written on December 19, 1993, about my daughter, Christine (Johnson) Morrison. It should be read, rather than my telling my reason for my writing it. The reason will be obvious after reading it.

<u>My Grownup Daughter</u>

My "little girl" didn't come home last night.
I was listening each hour to hear
Her words, "Mom, I'm home," which mean, "I'm all right;
Just letting you know I'm here."

But each hour that passed, brought not a sound
From that little girl of mine.
Only an echoing, "She's not coming 'round,"
Kept creeping into my mind.

I've listened for her since the day she was born,
From whimpers to a loud screaming bawl!
She'd come to our bed till her bad dream was gone.
Then I'd take her back down the hall.

As she grew older and went out at night,
I'd just have to pray to God
That He'd keep her safe till she came home all right;
And then I'd say, "Thank you, Lord."

But last night was long; I woke up a lot
Every hour, it seems.
And the same voice kept saying, "No, she is not
Coming home like in your dreams."

What is the reason that she stayed away
The reason it happened so soon?
My little girl grew up, married yesterday,
And left on her honeymoon.

I cannot believe that she grew up so fast,
The way I had always been told.
It feels as though such a short time has passed,
And now I am feeling old.

So all I can do now to get through the night
Is to place both of them in God's hand,
And pray that He'll keep them safe and all right
As, together, they live in God's plan.

"Mom, I'm Home"

"Mom, I'm home," are three short words
A mother needs to hear
In the middle of the night
From those whom she holds dear.

Her children fail to understand
When they're out late at night,
That till their mother knows they're home,
She hardly rests a mite.

She needs to know they're safely home
Where no harm will abound;
So till she hears these three short words,
She's apt to pace around.

This doesn't stop when they are grown
And visit home again.
Her instinct keeps her half awake
Till they are safely in.

If her children fuss too much,
She simply has to say,
"Be patient. This I cannot change.
Our Lord made me this way.

"He built this need into us all
When He created mothers.
I need to know that you are safe
You, your sisters, and brothers.

"And when at last I'm with the Lord,
When earthly life has ceased,
In HEAVEN hearing, 'Mom, I'm HOME,'
Then I can rest in peace."

"How can we get there, Mom?" they ask;
And this is her reply:
"You must believe in Jesus
Who for your sins did die.

"You must admit you're a sinner,
And ask Him your sins to forgive.
You must believe He arose from death
So that you will eternally live.

"You must believe He is knocking,
And invite Him into your heart.
This is the way to Heaven where
Believing loved ones never part."

A Mother Needs To Know

A mother needs to know
That her baby is all right
Any time of day
And any time of night.

When her baby's sleeping,
A mother tiptoes in
To make sure he's okay
And tiptoes out again.

When her child is older
And starts to toddle about,
She wants to keep him safe
As he goes in and out.

Then he's off to school--
It has to be that way.
For her, it's such a very
Sad and lonely day.

Then, when he's a teen,
Going out alone,
She can hardly sleep
Until he's safe at home.

A mother needs to know
That she has raised her child
To know and love the Lord
Who loves him all the while.

The love that Jesus gives him--
No greater love could be--
He took our sins upon Himself
As He died upon that tree.

A mother needs to know
That her son's been shown the way
To be at peace with God.
For this she'll always pray.

He must admit that
He has a spiritual need,
Admit that he's a sinner
While he is on his knees.
He must believe that Jesus died
On the cross for him,
Took his sins upon Himself
To forgive him of his sins.

He must repent and be willing
To turn away from sin,
To pray and open his heart--
Invite Lord Jesus in.

A mother needs to know
The day that her son starts
To really love the Lord
And invites Him into his heart.

He must then be baptized,
A command that's given by God,
To take a public stand
That Jesus is his Lord.

He then should join a church
Of Bible believers, indeed,
Folks who flock together
With Jesus at their lead.

A church is like a fire
With many a burning coal;
But pluck one out and leave it,
It soon dies and turns cold.

It needs the warmth of others
To be rekindled into fire.
And Christians need each other.
As they gather, they inspire.

Then, when her son's a man,
Starting his own life,
A mother needs to know
He'll choose a Christian wife.

When these two have children,
A mother needs to know
Their spirits will be nourished
As in the Lord they grow.

Before her life is ending,
A mother needs to know
Her children are believers
While she's still here below.

She needs to know she's told them
Of Jesus--the Life, Truth and Way--
That they'll live on forever
Because by Jesus they've been saved.

A mother needs to know that,
When she's in Heaven above,
Her children all will be there
Along with all she loves.

And, with this special knowledge,
When life's about to cease,
A mother then can know
That she can rest in peace.

Our Adult Child

When our child is grown, we love her no less
Than when she was a tiny tot.
We still have the longing to hold her close
Because we love her a lot.

But we must be careful to not interfere
With her in her adult life,
For now it's her spouse whom she needs the most
As it should be with husband and wife.

We spent years in raising our own child so dear;
And now that she is all grown,
She has her own husband who loves her a lot
And a family of her own.

While it's a real comfort to know that she's loved,
At times it is also quite hard
To stand back and let her be on her own.
We have to stay on our guard.

When she was a child and she'd gotten hurt
While having fun at play,
She would run to us for comfort and care,
And we'd love her hurt away.

But now, when she may be in trouble or pain,
For us it is doubly trying
To wait and to wonder if she is all right.
It is hard to keep from crying.

All we can do is to wait and to pray
And place her in God's arms.
He'll hold her close and carry her through
Her problems and keep her from harm.

So, Father, I place her once more in Your arms.
Please hold her as close as can be;
And, Father, I pray, when I can't be with her,
Dear Lord, please love her for me.

Her Baby's Tiny Hands

While pregnant with her son
Beneath her heart within,
She'd often feel his hands
Moving inside her skin.

He'd stretch his arm and hand,
And push out on her side.
She'd lovingly push it back
With a smile so sweet and
wide.

She could hardly wait
For his upcoming birth
To touch his tiny hands
And welcome him to Earth.

Then it finally came--
The night that he was born.
With joy she couldn't contain,
She held him until morn.

She explored his tiny fingers.
She counted all his toes.
She wanted to get to know
him--
His ears, his cheeks, his nose.

The wonder of it all,
At this new baby boy!
She could not hold back.
She wept with tears of joy.

She touched his tiny hand,
A miniature of his own.
He squeezed it tight on her
finger.
Such joy she had never
known!

The time passed and he grew.
As a toddler, it was grand
To walk along and hold
His fleshy little hand.

She taught him many things
Together they spent hours.
She'd take his little hand
And touch it to a flower.

When she would hold him
close,
He soon developed the knack
Of hugging her 'round the
neck,
His tiny hand patting her back.

As her son grew older,
His young hands also grew.
He learned many ways to use
them
Each day brought something
new.

She helped him learn to read.
She helped him learn to write.
Then, as the day was ending,
She'd pray with him at night.

He learned to use a hammer
With which to drive a nail.
He'd sometimes strike his
finger
And let out quite a wail!

Her son continued growing
And soon became a man.
She loved him just as much
As when his life began.

His hands were now full
grown--
So strong, yet tender, when
He, with deep compassion,
Comforted a friend.

She was extremely grateful
When his hands he would
fold;

And, bowing his head in
prayer,
To his Father in Heaven he'd
hold.

As the years flew swiftly by,
She watched her son with
pride--
His strong but gentle arms
And hands there at his side.

She then thought her life was
over!
She suffered unspeakable loss
When her son's beloved hands
Were nailed to a wooden
cross......

But that was just the
beginning,
For he died and rose again!
Her sorrow then was ended,
And joy replaced her pain.

For, you see, her son was
Jesus,
God coming to earth as man,
To save us from our sins
According to His plan.

We cannot save ourselves.
Our sins would lead to death.
God put our sins on Jesus,
The perfect and the best.

With this came our forgiveness
If we believe in Him
And ask Him into our hearts,
He'll take away our sins.

As He was resurrected,
Eternal Life He'll bring
To all who have faith, believe,
And to His hands will cling.

What Happened to Mama?

What happened to Mama
When I turned two?
She used to love everything
I would do.

But Mama has changed,
The one I once knew.
She doesn't always like
The things that I do.

Mama always loved
What I did before,
And she would always
Beg for more.

Now she keeps yelling.
She's not like before.
What will happen to Mama
When I turn four?

When I was born,
She was really sweet.
She wouldn't stop kissing
My tiny feet.

But, at two, these feet
Belong to me,
And they take me where
I want to be!

Mama always loved
My tiny hands
That now taunt the cat.
Why won't she understand?

Why's she so mad
When I pull the dog's tail?
I like it when
He lets out a wail!

Mama needs to know:
Independence I'm gaining;
But my love for her
Is surely not waning.

God made me this way.
There's nothing I can do.
I hope Mama still loves me
When I'm no longer two!

Please Don't Lie to Children

The most important night of the year
Should be filled with joy and cheer.
It's the night when God came down to earth
In the form of a Babe: Christ Jesus' birth.

He lived and died, our sins to forgive,
So we might all eternally live.
It's such an important Holy night
Which we have spoiled. It isn't right!

We've substituted Santa Claus
As the most special man that ever was.
For this, our Lord must surely grieve
Because, in Him, we do not believe.

And it must hurt Him even more
That we lie to children whom He adores.
We celebrate His birth with lies
To innocent children with hope-filled eyes.

They look to us and give their trust,
And we betray their faith in us.
How can we teach them not to lie
When we tell them that reindeer fly?

How can we tell them that Santa comes
Bringing toy soldiers, dolls and drums?
Our Lord tells us that we must not lie;
But, on His birthday, we lie and lie.

We not only lie about Santa Claus,
We omit Whose birth the first Christmas was.
So, let's renew their faith in us;
And be the people that children can trust.

"Don't Do As I Do."

There's an old saying
Heard along the way:
"Don't do as I do.
Do as I say."

This saying that's mentioned
Is one that's been heard
By many a child
From parents' own words.

But the words of the saying
Do not seem right,
For children copy parents
From morning till night.

They watch what we're doing
All the day long.
They learn from our actions
And follow along.

They hear what we're saying
And watch what we do,
And they notice the difference
Between the two.

There's a tendency for children
To follow the "wrong,"
So parents must be cautious
All their lives long.

If we don't want them shouting,
Then we must not shout.
It's then we must teach them
How to work things out.

If we don't want them fighting,
Then we must not fight;
And we must keep teaching them
Wrong from right.

If we don't want them lying,
Then we must not lie.
We must tell the truth
Or the fib they will spy.
What they are learning
From us now and here
Is how they'll be acting
In just a few years.

As teens they'll be acting
The way that we do.
All of our bad traits
In them will come through.

If we don't want them speeding,
Then we should not speed.
They'll watch what we do.
Our words they won't heed.

We must also be cautious
Of things that we read,
For they will be watching
And copy us indeed.

We must also be careful
Watching movies and T.V.,
For they will be doing
The bad things they see.

If we don't want them smoking,
Then we should not smoke.
We shouldn't be telling
Inappropriate jokes.

If we don't want them taking
Drugs and alcohol,
We must not take them either.
Into those traps they'll fall.

To teach them good morals,
All through their life,
We must set the example
As husband and wife.

If we don't want them stealing,
Then we must not steal.
Bringing things home from work
Is theft that is real.

If we want them to love,
We must show them the way
In the ways that we act,
Not just things that we say.

God gave us the guidelines
When He gave the Golden Rule,
Which says, "Do unto others
As you would have them do to you."

A Good Lesson For A Child

Each year we come together,
Our entire family,
And we all gather around
Our special Christmas tree.

We sing "Happy Birthday" to Jesus.
The children can hardly wait
To blow out all of the candles
And eat His birthday cake.

Before we open our presents,
We remember Jesus' birth
By reading from the Bible about
The night He came to earth.

Then I pick up Jesus in His manger
From beneath the Christmas tree
And tell the children the story
Of His love for them and for me.

I tell them we must love Him,
Believe in Him and be reborn,
And tell everyone about Him;
So I ask them to pass Him on.

We then pass the manger around
From one person to another--
Accepting Jesus and passing Him to
Each father, mother, sister and brother.

As my grandson had his turn today,
He was embarrassed to the core
When Baby Jesus slipped out of the manger
And landed on the floor!

The room was hushed with silence.
Not a single word was spoken.
Each person there was fearing that
The Baby Jesus figure was broken.

Then, when it was decided
That Baby Jesus was okay,
I told my grandson to pick Him up
And place Him back in the hay.

The room filled with laughter and relief
That everything was all right,
But my grandson was still so embarrassed
That he wanted to take flight.

He looked up into my eyes
As if for comfort he was pleading.
In that moment I definitely knew
That the Holy Spirit was leading.

I was then encouraged to tell him
The best advice I could give.
I told him, "Jesus would say,
'It's okay. I forgive.'"

A radiant smile burst forth when
Those words reached his little ears.
I saw such relief on his face.
He was no longer close to tears.

I pray that he learned this good lesson
To remember as long as he lives
Of how wonderful he'll always feel
When he hears Jesus say, "I forgive."

When the Children Come Home

When our children are young,
We can hardly wait
For them to come home
After being out late.

Then, when they are married
With children of their own,
We can still hardly wait
For them to come home.

But they are very busy
With their own families
And haven't much time
For their father and me.

But that is all right
Because we understand.
When they have time to come,
It makes us feel grand.

Right now, they are only
Together once a year;
And it is on Christmas
That they all gather here.

That day is for us
A day filled with joy--
To have them all together
With their own girls and boys.

But they won't realize
The joy we have known
Until their adult children
Once more gather at home.

Then they'll understand
The greatest hope of living
Is that they and their children
Will be together in Heaven.

The way for this to happen
Is to ask Jesus into their hearts,
So they all will live in Heaven where
Believing loved ones never part.

RIGHT TO LIFE

On February 28, 1988, my pregnant daughter, Marcia, and her husband, Jeff, were visiting us. She and I were sitting beside each other on the sofa when she said, "Mom, do you want to feel the baby move?" Of course I did! She took my hand and placed it on the spot where she had felt the baby move. After waiting a few seconds, sure enough, I felt a little pressure on the palm of my hand. The rest of the day I could still remember the pressure and feel the warmth on the spot where that little baby had touched my hand through my daughter's skin. That night I was praying and thanking God for that feeling which was still on my palm and for the baby who was being formed in my daughter's womb. As I prayed and pondered these feelings, a poem started flowing into my thoughts. This poem came so rapidly and, since I am not a poet, I decided I had better get out of bed and write it down so I would be able to remember it in the morning. These are the words I was given that night.

To My Unborn Grandchild

Today's the day I felt your touch!
I'd known that it would mean so much.
Your mother felt you move within
And placed my hand upon her skin.

I waited, oh so patiently,
And then I felt your little knee.
Perhaps it was your foot or hand.
Whatever it was, it sure felt grand!

I feel it still! I feel it yet!
It's something I shall not forget.
The feeling that was so divine
You life's warmth on this palm of mine.

God is so good! God is so great!
He knew that I could hardly wait.
This special time He gave us three:
My own first born, her child, and me.

On June 25, 1994, our daughter, Marcia, and her husband, Jeff, came to tell us that they were expecting their second child. Because they had had two previous miscarriages, they waited to tell anyone until they could have an ultrasound of the baby eight weeks into the pregnancy. They brought the ultrasound with them when they told us about the baby. They gave us pictures of the ultrasound to keep. That night, this poem formed in my mind. I had no idea that the joy of this day would turn to such sadness, when seven weeks later, this baby would be miscarried, as well.

To My Unborn Second Grandchild

On June 24 I met you
In picture form so soon.
I never will forget you
Resting in your mother's womb.

I had no way of knowing
That you were on your way.
For eight weeks you've been growing
Oh, what a happy day!

Your tiny precious form
Was such a joy to see
Snuggled safe and warm
It filled my heart with glee!

I just can't wait to hold you
On the day of your coming birth.
Till then, may God's love enfold you
As it will all your days on earth.

Why Does "Goodness" Have to Die?

As I pause to think, I'm wondering why...
Why does all "goodness" have to die?
All of the good things that we once had
Are nowadays thought of as being bad.

When I think of the "goodness" of family,
I miss the way that it used to be:
A husband and wife working side by side,
With children born for them to guide.

When God created the human race,
Each one in the family had his place.
A father and mother neither alone,
Both needed by children in every home.

A male and a female are part of God's plan
Not woman with woman, nor man with man.
Not one of God's creatures did He create
To take one of its own sex to be its mate.

The "goodness" of children is being destroyed
Abortion killing millions of girls and boys.
All of these babies, who yet are unborn,
Out of their mothers' wombs being torn.

When I think about the "goodness" of life,
So quickly snuffed out with a bullet or knife
Respect for life is fast slipping away.
We're hearing more about it each day.

People deciding who lives and who dies,
Are totally wrong in God's holy eyes.
These choices of life are not ours to make.
Life is God given and His alone to take.

God gave us such blessings, it must hurt Him so
To see how we're letting so much "goodness" go.
The way that we're living must make His heart break,
But I know that He loves us in spite of this ache.

For, as I think back to Calvary,
When the "Ultimate Goodness" died on that tree
For the forgiveness of sinners like me and like you,
Christ said, "Father, forgive them; for they know not what they do."

And, because He loved us, our Savior arose!
His love and forgiveness He continually bestows.
If we will repent and in Jesus believe,
Eternal Life is the peace we'll receive.

In order to know this, remember the thief,
Who, while on the cross, expressed his belief.
Jesus' answer to him just before the thief dies:
"Today you will be with me in paradise."

There was a segment about abortion on the 6:00 evening news on January 26, 1993. It showed a sterile operating room with a bright, shiny pail at the foot of the table. The news segment was pointing out that all abortions aren't performed in such nice surroundings. The news reporter was trying to say that legalized abortions are performed in nice, clean, sterilized rooms like this one and were more desirable than illegal ones.

That pail really bothered me. I was finally able to get to sleep but was awakened at 4 a.m. with the following poem which again, simply flowed from my pen onto the paper as quickly as I could write it down.

I wrote this, not to get into the realm of legality (anti-abortion vs. pro-choice), but to appeal to young women, doctors and nurses to not have or perform abortions. This should not be decided by the government. We should look into our own hearts and consciences and know how morally wrong and tragic it is.

The Bright, Shiny Pail

Look! I'm a shiny new pail!
I'm round, two feet tall, with a bail.
Just off the assembly line,
I'm polished and brilliantly shine.

Stainless steel, I was made in a mold.
Wow! What does my future hold?
My friends are all shiny and new.
I wonder if they're happy, too.

Someone who's strong and able
Puts me at the foot of a table.
This seems like a good place to be.
I wonder how they will use me.

This room is so shiny and clean;
Everything's polished to a sheen.
In a country that's been "civilized,"
I'm proud to be all sterilized.

My job seems about to begin!
A nurse and a doctor walk in.
So excited, my heart starts to pound!
Next to me the doctor sits down.

What's this! Oh, no! It can't be!
What are they putting in me?
Dear God, get me out of that door!
This can't be what I was made for!

On a table a young girl is lying.
She's whimpering and she's crying.
Into me, the doctor drops "parts":
Tiny fingers, tiny toes, a tiny heart - - - -

Dear God, may these people repent.
For sinners, Jesus was sent.
Your forgiveness and peace they'll need
To live with this terrible deed.

In case they do not know the way,
They must get on their knees and pray,
And ask You their sins to forgive.
You'll accept them and help them to live

Endangered Species

Our world is so concerned,
And rightfully so,
About all the species
As they're about to go.

The species that God gave us--
The list goes on and on--
If we do not preserve them,
They surely will be gone.

We prevent construction
And leave the land alone
For an endangered bird
Which calls this land his home.

We protect the pandas
In a zoo both night and morn,
And everyone rejoices
When their baby panda's born.

Buffaloes were hunted
For hides and sport. I think
Because of all this killing,
The buffalo's nearly extinct.

Elephants being slaughtered
For their ivory tusks
Has lowered their numbers.
To save them, we must.

We "Brake for Animals"
That are crossing the road.
We don't want to hurt them
As on their way they go.

We "Protect the Whales"
Whose numbers were waning.
By protecting them,
Their population is gaining.

We "Save the Seals"
With their eyes big and round.
We don't want them clubbed
As they cower on the ground.

We can't look upon
The violence of these kills
Without our stomachs churning
And starting to feel ill.

But our most important species
That we are letting go
Doesn't seem to phase us
As we go to and fro.

We do not see the violence
When they are being killed.
Some don't even think it's wrong.
Many people never will.

For we have been persuaded
To kill our girls and boys
While they're safe in their mother's womb,
Because it is her "choice".

But our Savior hates abortion!
It's certainly not His will!
We may become an endangered species,
For He said, "Thou shalt not kill."

For you who have had abortions
In the years before,
If you'll come to Him filled with sorrow,
He'll say, "Go and sin no more."

For Jesus came to save us sinners.
As He hung upon that cross,
It was for our forgiveness
So we would not be lost.

Think of the Joy

Think of the joy you are feeling.
The racing of your heart is wild.
Your adult daughter has just told you
She is pregnant with her first child.

You grab her, and you hug her.
Your thoughts rush back to when
She was your own dear baby
As you hold her close again.

You remember the incredible joy
When they placed her in your arms.
Never wanting to let her go,
You'd protect her from all harm.

She's now grown into a woman
With a baby growing within.
You can hardly wait to feel it
Moving beneath her skin.

You can't wait to tell your friends
The sweetest news of all,
That you are expecting a grandchild.
You'll tell everyone who calls!

You can't wait to be a grandparent.
You're already making plans
For the fun you'll have with your grandchild
While you hold that little hand.

You think of all the fun things
The two of you can do
And all the things that you can teach,
Like tying a little shoe,

Like listening to a bird singing,
Or picking a flower for Mom,
And learning to hit a baseball--
The list goes on and on.

Think of the joy when this grandchild
Is baptized and dedicated to God,
When this life with all of its meaning
Is given back to the Lord.

You can hardly wait for this grandchild,
Just beginning to grow in place,
That tiny body well formed;
But you've several more months to wait.

You must wait until you hold the baby
For the greatest joy you will feel--
For the awe of this beautiful grandchild.
You can hardly believe it's all real!

Now think of the agony you are feeling!
You're now suffering a broken heart
Because your daughter's next statement
Is tearing your soul apart!

She simply does not want her baby,
Her precious girl or boy;
And nothing you say will change her mind
Because it is her "choice".....

The only thing you can do
Is pray to our Lord in your need,
For your daughter will need His forgiveness
If she proceeds with this terrible deed.

And soon she will realize
That her agony will not cease.
Only God's grace and forgiveness
Will provide her with any peace.

In the late winter and early spring of 2006, I was happily writing introductions to all of my poems when I came to this one. It has been two weeks since I wrote my last introduction because this one is very painful to remember and to write about. I had written this poem during the night of August 9, 1994, after our daughter, Marcia, and her husband, Jeff, had lost a third baby to miscarriage at fifteen weeks into her pregnancy. I had put the poem in a folder that I had titled, "Unfinished," and never re-read it or showed it to anyone in the nearly twelve years since it was written. Since I am writing my introductions in chronological order, this is the next one to be written. When I went to the folder and read the poem, I found that it was indeed finished, only needing a title and needing to be typewritten. I have been putting off writing this introduction for two weeks, but now it is time to write it.

On August 9, 1994, Ernie and I were living in Massachusetts and were planning to drive to Portland, ME, to take our son, Dean, out for lunch because it was his 27th birthday. After Dean had gone to work, Jeff called us from the hospital in Nashua, NH, saying that Marcia had lost the baby that she was carrying. We told him that we would be there as soon as possible. We hung up the phone and tried to reach Dean at work to tell him what had happened and that we would not be able to take him out for lunch. We couldn't reach him because he was not available. We kept trying until we left for NH and then continued trying to reach him when we got there. I can't remember how we finally got in touch with him. I think we probably asked our daughter, Christine, who was living in Maine, to keep trying to reach him. Anyway, he finally called us at the hospital. Christine and her husband, Kevin, had also driven to the hospital. When we arrived, Marcia and Jeff were in their room. On the table beyond the foot of the bed was a white towel. Marcia told us that the baby was wrapped inside it and asked us if we wanted to see her. We all hesitated briefly, not knowing what to do. Then I stepped forward and pulled the towel open, one corner at a time. We all looked at the tiny, six-inch-long, perfectly formed fifteen-week-old fetus (truly a <u>baby</u>) lying there. We cried together and wrapped the blanket back around the baby. We spent the day at the hospital. Marcia and Jeff's minister of Grace Lutheran Church in Nashua, Pastor Michael Meyer, came to be with them. He had been quite a distance away at a week-long camping experience with a group of young people from their church; but he left there to be with Marcia and Jeff, which meant so much to them. After he had left, the baby had been taken downstairs in the hospital to be taken care of in some manner. Marcia and Jeff were torn apart about not knowing what would become of the baby. Ernie was out of the room and, when he came back, I whispered to him what was happening. We all agreed that we should call down there and tell them to hold the baby there until we could make some arrangements. Ernie took it upon himself to call someone in the phone book to see if the baby could have a proper burial. The person that he reached put him in touch with someone at a cemetery in Lowell, MA. The told him that they didn't usually have burials for babies under twenty weeks, but they would make an exception. We were told that the baby should be named and then could be buried in the "Garden of Angels" section for babies in that cemetery. Marcia and Jeff were trying to decide on a name. A name came to me and I asked if they might want to call her Angel. They both liked that and agreed on it. They then chose Grace as a middle name after their Grace Lutheran Church. They then made plans with their minister to hold a funeral service for her a few days later in a Chapel at the cemetery. Marcia asked me if I could make a little blanket for the baby to be wrapped in inside the tiny white casket. I agreed and that night I went to the fabric store and found some beautiful light blue fabric with the color of the sky, clouds and little Precious Moments angels on each cloud. I bought yellow lace and made the tiny blanket with lace around it to wrap her in. I later made little bookmarks from the same fabric and lace and gave them to Marcia and Jeff, Ernie's and my parents, Jeff's parents, his brothers, and to our Dean and Christine, and kept one for ourselves in Angel's memory.

On the night that we got home from the hospital, I couldn't get to sleep. I finally got up and put my thoughts on paper in the form of the following poem, which I put in the folder and hadn't read in nearly twelve years until today. Just as I had dreaded, I am now emotionally drained after re-living this time in our lives. I am doing it, however, in the prayer that it will help someone else who may be going through a similar experience. I am also praying that it may prevent one or many people from aborting their own babies, or help them to receive God's forgiveness and peace if they have already done so.

__If You Could See What I Saw__

If you could see what I saw today,
I know your heart would ache.
If you could see what I saw today,
I know your heart would break.

I saw my tiny granddaughter,
A fetus, fifteen weeks old,
Lying there wrapped in a towel,
Her tiny body stone cold.

Her beautiful little six-inch-long form
Was a baby, there's no doubt,
Complete with each of her parts in place
Waiting to grow and at full term come out.

Her little arms were folded
Across her tiny chest.
Every finger and toe was there
Along with all the rest.

Her tiny little face had the shape
Of her six-year-old sister's face.
God had been knitting her together
With everything in place.

Her father and mother wanted her so,
But it wasn't meant to be.
The miscarriage broke both their hearts.
It's really tough to see.

It really makes me furious
When I think of how someone could take
The life of one of these babies--
Oh, how my heart does ache.

Millions and millions of women
Are being scammed each day
By being told that these are not babies--
Just "tissue" to be tossed away.

If they could see what I saw today
I know their tears would flow.
Never again could they ever doubt
And I know that their faith would grow.

That tiny baby touched our lives
As only a baby can.
Please don't destroy one of your own.
Each one is a part of God's plan.

If perhaps, for you it's too late--
If you did it before you knew,
Repent and turn from your sins to Jesus.
He'll forgive you and help you get through.

On the morning of the funeral for our little fifteen-week-old fetal granddaughter, Angel, this poem came to my thoughts. I quickly wrote it and made about twenty-five copies of it to be given to people at the funeral. Before the funeral began, Marcia and Jeff were alone in a room at the cemetery. I went in and showed it to them and told them they could have it read at the service if they chose to. They read it and decided it would be too difficult for them to hear it read there. I then asked them if they minded if I passed them out to people there and they said that would be all right. I was told later by a family friend whose son and his wife had lost a child at birth, that the poem was very helpful to them. This is the poem that follows.

Angel Grace Newell

Precious fetal granddaughter of mine,
You entered Heaven on August 9.
Your life on earth not meant to be
You're now with God eternally.

In your short life, we loved you so.
It started when we came to know
That you were coming, on your way.
We didn't know you couldn't stay...

We named you little Angel Grace.
In our hearts, you'll have a special place.
You've touched our lives, though we feel pain.
Fifteen weeks in the womb, were not lived in vain.

This hurt we cannot understand,
But we know you're safe now in God's hand.
And thanks to Him, He heals our pain
With the promise that we shall meet again.

Nowhere to Hide

One day everything was peaceful.
I was taking a nap,
Looking forward to the time when
I'd be snuggled on my mother's lap.

I was needing lots of sleep
And protection from all harm.
I was needing to gain my strength
In a place that was safe and warm.

I was growing a little stronger
And a little taller each day,
Wondering in my young mind
About how much I now weighed.

I didn't have any worries.
I didn't have any fears.
Everything was peaceful.
I never shed any tears.

Everything here was secure.
I was safe in my tiny room.
All of my needs were provided.
I was in my mother's womb!

But all of a sudden it came--
Something prodding my side.
It hurt and I started kicking.
I tried to find somewhere to hide!

No matter how much I fought it,
No matter how much I cried,
It twisted, crumpled and sucked me in;
And at that moment I died!

In Psalm 139 it is written that
God knit me together in the womb;
But, because of what was done to me,
My mom's womb became my tomb!

Dear Lord,
    For some people who've made mistakes
    In the choices they have made,
    Help them know that their sins You'll forgive
    If at the foot of the cross they're laid.
        In Jesus' name I pray, Amen.

162

Oh, How I Wish We Had Known

We were so young and afraid,
Aware of the bad choice we'd made.
Not knowing where to turn,
The consequences we soon would learn.

Out of wedlock, we had conceived,
Which neither of us could believe.
We didn't know what to do
And had no one that we could turn to.

We gathered some money and went
To a place where a friend had sent.
We entered a small, dark room.
The scene was one of gloom.

In a short while, it was done.
The three of us, now minus one.
But, wait, there is no relief!
Only sickening guilt and grief.

Oh no! What did we do?
There's no one that we can turn to.
Why are we feeling so sad
Instead of relieved and glad?

We don't know if we'll ever be able
To forget what was done on that table.
How can we possibly go on
While regretting it night and morn?

It will haunt us the rest of our life,
Even if we're husband and wife.
How we're yearning for peace of mind
Which we're afraid we will never find.

Now, years later, with nowhere to turn
To find peace for which we still yearn,
We hear about God up above
Offering peace, forgiveness and love.

Jesus came for sinners who are lost
To die in our place on the cross.
If we will repent and believe,
He'll forgive and give us His peace.

How I wish we had known
That we couldn't make it alone.
With Jesus by our side,
He'll be our Comfort and Guide.

163

Torn into Pieces

As a loud thunderstorm began,
I quickly went out on our deck
To retrieve some shoes from there
So that they would not get wet.

In doing so, I startled
Two animals down below
Who started running away
Just as fast as they could go.

The animal running ahead
Was a tiny chipmunk so cute.
It was obvious he'd lose the race
With a stray cat in pursuit.

As I went back into the house,
I could hear the horrible screams.
I heard them the rest of the night
Only in my mind and my dreams.

The little chipmunk was screaming
As he was being torn apart,
While the cat was happily devouring
His legs, his stomach, his heart....

My mind then switched to babies
In mothers' wombs being torn apart
By suction tubes or scissors - -
Tiny fingers, tiny toes, tiny heart.

We know that these babies feel
The terrible, excruciating pain.
Seen on ultrasounds, they try to escape
The torture again and again.

Dear Lord, let people wake up
To the reality of this crime - -
It's one of the most terrible acts
That is happening all the time.

And, dear God, let them understand
That, if they repent of their sin,
You will help them to live
With a clean slate on which to begin.

In the Living Bible, Matthew 1:18 to 1:25 states:

This is how the birth of Jesus the Messiah came about. His mother Mary and Joseph had promised to get married. But before they started to live together, it became clear that she was going to have a baby. She became pregnant by the power of the Holy Spirit. Her husband Joseph was faithful to the law. But he did not want to put her to shame in public. So he planned to divorce her quietly.

But as Joseph was thinking about this, an angel of the Lord appeared to him in a dream. The angel said, "Joseph, son of David, don't be afraid to take Mary home as your wife. The baby inside her is from the Holy Spirit. She is going to have a son. You must give him the name Jesus. That's because he will save his people from their sins."

All this took place to bring about what the Lord had said would happen. He had said through the prophet, "The virgin is going to have a baby. She will give birth to a son. And he will be called Immanuel." The name Immanuel means "God with us."

Joseph woke up. He did what the angel of the Lord commanded him to do. He took Mary home as his wife. But he did not sleep with her until she gave birth to a son. And Joseph gave him the name Jesus.

What If?

What if they both were frightened?
What if they didn't believe?
What if they both were embarrassed
To tell others how she had conceived?

What if they suddenly decided
That the embarrassment they couldn't endure?
What if they chose to abort Him?
The "What ifs" were beginning to lure.

But, praise God, they both were faithful.
She gave birth to the Son of God.
Today they are still held most high
Because on the right path they trod.

All of us humans are sinners.
Although some sins seem hard to erase,
If we ask Jesus, He'll forgive us;
For He died on the cross in our place.

To my friends and loved ones,

As I think about my life, I ask myself, "What is the best gift that I can give my loved ones and friends while I am here on earth and after I have gone to be with the Lord?"

When we find a good recipe, we want to cook it for our loved ones. When we see a good movie, we want to share it with our loved ones. When we eat at a really nice restaurant, we want to encourage our loved ones to eat there. When we see a beautiful lake or mountain, we want our loved ones to see it, as well. I think many of you know that what I want most to share with you is the gift of peace that came into my life when I accepted Jesus as my Lord and Savior. When I learned in Romans 3:23, "For all have sinned and fall short of the glory of God," I finally understood my feelings of guilt and unworthiness -- always trying to please the Lord and always feeling that I had failed Him. When I finally learned that He loves me just as I am, in fact, so much that He sent His Son, Jesus, to die on the cross in my place for the forgiveness of my sins if I would only believe in Him, I could hardly contain my Joy! When I told Him I was sorry for my sins and asked Him to come into my heart, He lifted my burden of guilt about always striving and failing to please Him,and replaced it with peace and joy beyond words.

My reason for writing this and for always being concerned for the salvation of all those I know and love, is a lesson I learned many years ago in Bible Study. The story was told of a person who was in Heaven and saw his loved ones being turned away. They turned to him and said, "Why didn't you tell us?" That story touched me deeply and has been moving me ever since.

Jesus said in John 14:6, "I am the way, the truth and the life: no man cometh unto the Father, but by me." Our role as Christians is to tell everyone. I try to tell the world through my poems and my writing. I want to make sure I tell my loved ones, and I pray that their hearts will be open to receiving this gift of God's peace -- the "peace that passes all understanding." He's standing, knocking and waiting at the door of our hearts to be invited in. He will not force His way in. We must open the door. In order to invite Him in, to be saved, and to receive His peace, we need to pray something like this:

> "Dear God, I realize that I am a sinner who is unable to save myself. I am sorry for all of my sins. Thank you for sending Jesus, Who took my sins upon Himself and died on the cross in my place for the forgiveness of my sins, so that I might have eternal life in Heaven with You. I turn from my sins and invite You into my heart to be my Lord and Savior. In Jesus' name, Amen."

After doing this, we will have given ourselves and our loved ones the greatest gift that we can ever give them -- the knowledge that we will be living eternally in Heaven. God doesn't promise to save our bodies, but He does promise to save our souls. When our loved ones stand at our grave, they can have the peace in knowing that we are not in that grave, but are living on in Heaven with Jesus. What greater gift can we give them? And no greater gift can our loved ones give us than by telling us that they also believe in Jesus, which means we will all be living together forever in Heaven.

This is the gift that I want so much to give to my loves ones and to each of you who reads this. My prayer is that you will share this gift with your loved ones, as well.

Printed in the United States
By Bookmasters